*Nov. 2008*

*To Iain*

*May God Bless*
*You Through*

# Window of Hope...
# and Reconciliation

*2 Cors: 18-20*

*Donald _____*

*Ps 122: 8, 9*

# Window
# of Hope...
## and Reconciliation

Donald Gingras

PUBLISHING

Belleville, Ontario, Canada

# WINDOW OF HOPE... AND RECONCILIATION
### Copyright © 2008, Donald Gingras

Scriptures marked NIV are from *The Holy Bible, New International Version.* Copyright © 1973, 1978, 1984 International Bible Society. Used by permission of Zondervan Publishing House. All rights reserved. • Scriptures marked KJV are from *The Holy Bible, King James Version.* Copyright © 1977, 1984, Thomas Nelson Inc., Publishers.

ISBN : 978-1-55452-283-5 (English edition)
ISBN : 978-1-55452-325-2 (French edition)

Heart Cry for Quebec / Cri du Coeur pour le Québec
2137 Baldwin
Montréal, Québec, Canada, H1L 5A5
(514) 353-1131
www.ccquebec.org • www.hcquebec.org
E-mail: donald.gingras@videotron.ca

*Essence Publishing* is a Christian Book Publisher dedicated to furthering the work of Christ through the written word. For more information, contact:
20 Hanna Court, Belleville, Ontario, Canada K8P 5J2.
Phone: 1-800-238-6376. Fax: (613) 962-3055.
E-mail: info@essence-publishing.com
Web site: www.essence-publishing.com

Dedication

To my Quebec that I truly love.
To find its identity, an authentic freedom and full
meaning in life through this "window of hope"—
this is my "Heart Cry for Quebec!"

# TABLE OF CONTENTS

✠

# Foreword

—— ✠ ——

In the early spring of 2001, Donald Gingras and I were invited to Montreal, where a group was exploring the theme "What does Quebec need from the Rest of Canada?" Meeting on the way to the lunch room, we exchanged a few pleasantries; then my attention was galvanized by his assertion that the way forward for Quebec and the Rest of Canada (known as the RoC in polling) lies in reconciliation. In one of the forums earlier that morning, with the imagery of Hugh MacLennan's allegorical novel *Two Solitudes* in mind, I had briefly explored the idea of breaking down the dividing walls.

Enough was said to convince me that Donald should have a few minutes in a plenary session, and I proposed this to one of the organizers of the day. Donald got a brief spot in the summary segment. He made two points. One was that reconciliation re-establishes broken relationships. The other was that he, once an active separatist, was sorry to have caused pain for many in the RoC, and he asked forgiveness from those present in that room. Then he stood quietly for a moment. The room was equally quiet. Perhaps everyone, like me, was wondering what might need to happen next.

Just then the session chair (the organizer I had spoken with) seemed to realize the ball was in his court. He stepped towards Donald, and his unrehearsed response came forth. "Our attitudes have been judgmental, and we have distanced ourselves in response," he noted. "Sometimes our calloused humour at the expense of *les Québécois* has bordered on racism," he confessed. In extending our hearty forgiveness, "we too are equally in need of yours," he said, turning to Donald. There's more to the story, but I will leave you to imagine its ending.

Within two years, Donald and I found ourselves to be working colleagues, and our mandate has included things related to the theme of that day in Dorval. As an educator once pressed into the pleasant task of teaching Canadian history in a small international school where curriculum sometimes exceeded the staff's specialization, I found Donald's "take" on Quebec's history within Canada intriguing. One reason for Canada's two solitudes must be their differing perspectives on their shared history. Donald and I collaborated on a short joint paper touching Quebec, Canada, history and reconciliation. Soon Donald was convinced to develop that theme into a book. Here it is.

James McDowell
Kitchener, ON

# ACKNOWLEDGMENTS

❧

WITH MY WIFE LORRAINE, I TAKE THIS UNIQUE OPPORTUNITY TO express our heartfelt gratitude toward our parents for their love and the rich heritage of Judeo-Christian values they left us. I acknowledge the positive influence that Gilles Héroux, a priest and inspiring educator, had on me as a student in Juvénat St-Viateur boarding high school. We are also grateful to Simon Roy and Claude Vachon for their friendship and love for God's Word that led us to discover the path to reconciliation with God.

This book has been a challenging journey. The project started in 1988 as I moved my family to Caronport, Saskatchewan, to study for three wonderful years at Briercrest Bible College. Living there allowed us to learn a new perspective in relationships: reconciliation; this was a triggering experience that birthed this project. But I never thought it would lead me to write a book. Then Harold Lutzer, who showed so much love for us *Québécois*, never stopped encouraging me to write this story. I thank you people from Caronport for modelling a caring community; a sincere thank you to Ken and Judy Guenter, Dr. Carl and Della Handerager, Dr. Paul Magnus and my professor in counselling, Dr. Marv Penner. My warm appreciation to Dr. Bob Seal, my friend (and theologian), for his investment in my life and his precious comments while reviewing my book.

This book has been a genuine team effort. James McDowell, my writing coach, with unfailing patience and so generous with his time, never gave up on me to pursue excellence. I want to express how much I have benefitted from the wisdom and commitment of Dr. Rad Dzero and Marie-Andrée Gagnon in reviewing my manuscript. I also appreciate the precious counsel of Paul Gaumond, Jean Nicolas Laperle, Dr. Richard Lougheed, Jean-Louis Lalonde, Eileen Lageer and Dr. Allen Stouffer. In a broader sense, I extend my particular appreciation to the Canadian Revival Fellowship and the Evangelical Missionary Church of Canada, my mission organizations who allowed me the time needed for this project. I also thank our faithful partners and friends of Heart Cry for Quebec Network. My greatest gratitude must be expressed to my wife and faithful friend, Lorraine, for her commendable patience, consistent support and friendship through all this revealing and life-transforming journey. Finally, to our children and their spouses who walked with us positively all along the way, I reveal the full heart of a fulfilled father.

# PREFACE

For four years (2001-05) my wife, Lorraine, and I made lecture tours across Canada. Many invitations came in. We went from one city to another speaking to organizations, as well as in homes, schools and Christian congregations. We got to know people better as we accepted their call to come and peer at life through their window. During the three years we lived in Western Canada and through our several tours, we invested quality time discussing, reading and interviewing First Nation peoples, English Canadians, French Canadians living outside of Quebec and immigrants. We researched both Quebec's and Canada's history. It was a fruitful investment. Having learned so much about a French Canadian "child"—really an "orphan," wanting to be affirmed and liberated—one could discern more clearly who the *Québécois* are. Our appreciation of their religious and cultural heritage grew, and we saw its ancestral transmission from France and onwards from one generation to the next.

The *Québécois* have a sense of tradition that is unique in North America, to a degree that is difficult for their English-speaking neighbours to understand or appreciate. "No real understanding of French Canada is possible without the realization of what its history means."[1]

## A Shocking Discovery

Travelling across Canada, we were shocked at how so many Canadians outside of Quebec are unaware of what we French Canadians

13

really experienced in our relationships with France, with Roman Catholicism and through the Quiet Revolution. It is imperative that Canadians understand that the story of Quebec, the grown-up orphan, cannot be dissociated from the history of the Rest of Canada. The 400th anniversary of Quebec City (2008) recalls not only the foundation of Quebec City; modern Canada itself dates back to that event. From 1534 to 1760, French and English adventurers discovered, explored and then invaded the American land mass. Competing and fighting vehemently with each other, they used and damaged the "Indians" in their efforts to control the lucrative fur business. From Britain's 1759 Conquest of Quebec until now, after being irrevocably separated from his parent(s) and natural family (France), Quebec had no option but to live among both Native and English-speaking people. During the Quiet Revolution of the 1960s, Quebec, now a grown-up orphan, responding to the political and religious abuse and wounds he had experienced, expressed feelings of rebellion against both his Canadian blended family and his original family's Roman Catholic parish.

In the following chapters, I wholeheartedly invite you to join me in imagining some counselling sessions. The scenario will be this: the counsellee is a personified Quebec, who is a hurting child, living an orphan's life in some sort of a British "foster home" alongside Native children and their "eternal European enemies," the English children, who are natural children of this new blended family. Quebec is going through a time of questioning because of what he suffered; his life story is marked by ongoing and unresolved broken relationships. The grown-up orphan, Quebec, is dealing with pain while realizing his unhappy destiny to live in a Canada built through long, ongoing conflicts, in which his side eventually was the loser.

Since the British Conquest of 1759, Native, French and English Canadians have lived as a dysfunctional, hurting, blended family, carrying the painful heritage of a broken home in crisis. Indeed, too preoccupied by business, economy and political power, Canadians have learned to fight and to keep their distance from each other, minimizing the importance of relationships. The absence of compassion, care and respect in their differences demonstrate a deep lack of teaching and

14

coaching for genuine reconciliation. Now, with the addition of recently adopted children (immigrants), how can Canadians build healthy relationships in the midst of the existing unresolved broken relationships? One could ask, is there hope? A battle ensues in Quebec's mind—should he stay with the hurting Canadian blended family or leave?

In the following case study, the counsellor seeks to understand Quebec's feelings and reactions in the light of his life story, helping him confront his painful memories to experience healing. The counsellor asks Quebec to do some homework between sessions—to reflect deeply on his life, to recall "triggering historical events" that touch him as he reads, remembers and ponders earlier seasons of his life. Quebec will also be talking with his new friend Donald, considering the meaningful findings and insights Donald has from reading and researching the history of the Canadian blended family. From there Donald will challenge Quebec to take a fresh look at his problems from a new window. "Just as an individual would, so an entire community or people should endeavour to clarify their life story, and so begin to understand their identity."[2]

One result of our touring was that it helped to clarify why Quebec was driven toward wanting to be independent, to become *maître chez nous* ("master of its own destiny"), desiring to live apart from the Rest of Canada.

> Conquest, like slavery, must be experienced to be understood...One can intellectually perceive what it means, [but in experiencing it] the whole life structure of the conquered is laid open to his masters. [The conquered] become second-rate people. Wherever they turn, something meets their eyes to symbolize their subjection...As long as the French are French and the English are English [and the Native are Native], the memory of the conquest and its effect will remain.[3]

Another facet was that it shed light on the dramatic and spectacular drop of *Québécois* interest in and practice of the Roman Catholic faith in such a short period of time, starting at the 1960 Quiet Revolution. Finally, through our research and touring, we found out that many

European Christian religious traditions have been detrimental to the development of harmonious relationships between French, Native and English in North America.

During our tour, each time I related themes from this story, the outcome was eye opening. The thought patterns of many people concerning the broken relationships among French, Native and English were challenged or even transformed. One suggestion came over and over: "Get this story written; it helps so much to look at our history through this original window. It makes a difference to understand how politics, business and organized religion influenced our country. Canadians ought to hear this perspective."

The result is the book you have in your hands. In it you will learn what I experienced in Quebec as a French Catholic *Québécois* baby boomer. I was an altar boy, a teacher, a hockey coach...and a separatist! You will also read about a crossroad that transformed my life, through which I have been enabled to see and write this story from a new window (paradigm).

My purpose was not at all to write another book on history; I leave this to historians. To the contrary, it is possible for an informed reader to find simplistic the interpretation or importance we give to some historical events. But, from a window of family counselling, I applied myself to choosing specific triggering events in an attempt to help explain the challenging relationships among the three founding nations of the Canadian blended family in their historical social context up to now.

We hope the metaphor of the case study will help French, Native and English Canadians and new immigrants realize that the Canadian blended family dilemma is more than a problem of politics, power, money and land; it deals with a heritage of ongoing broken relationships. Indeed, the problem is deeply rooted in what French, Native and English have valued and treasured in their spirits and souls to make life work while they have been struggling in the Canadian ring.

The story is also designed for "personified Quebec" to get some strategic insights into the distinct society or nation he claims to be. It will provide key information for finding out how life works for him as well as understanding the thoughts gestating in his mind, the way he has been relating to others and the values driving his quest for fulfillment. Quebec will also realize how the parish- and priest-centred homogeneous society—"One language, one country and one religion"—in which he lived isolated from the rest of the world for several centuries in North America shaped his life and character. Quebec, whose mind and soul have been hurting for a long time, ends up facing a critical challenge that, if embraced, has the potential to heal and transform his life.

⚜ ————————————————

[1]   Mason Wade, *The French Canadians*: 1760–1945, p.1. The French historian referred to is Catholic Canon Lionel Groulx.

[2]   Raymond Lemieux and Jean-Paul Montminy, *Le catholicisme Québécois*, p. 10. Quoting Fernand Dumont, Genèse de la société Québécoise [Genesis of Quebec society], (Montreal: Boréal, 1993).

[3]   A.R.M. Lower, "Two Ways of Life: The Primary Antithesis of Canadian History." Essay featured in *Approaches to Canadian History*, pp. 18-19.

# INTRODUCTION

❧

## A NEW VENTURE

"Why do you want to leave Quebec and go thousands of miles away to live among English Canadians?" my friends asked me, some almost in tears. "And why would you want to start studying again at your age anyway? You are thirty-eight! We don't understand you."

It was true. I had disposed of my Montreal sports business. My wife and I sold our commercial building and with our children, Martin, ten, and Claudiane, eight, packed up for a move to Briercrest Bible College in Caronport, Saskatchewan, to be trained in biblical studies and family counselling. After paying our debts, we had just enough money left to live on during our first year there. It surely was going to be a challenging venture.

"What are you doing, Donald?" some asked. "You know that *Québécois* for centuries were absolutely forbidden by the clergy to even open a Bible, much less read it, and here you are—going away to study it! And in English! You don't even speak that language well."

Others were really bewildered. "How are you going to make a living while studying?" they asked.

"I expect I can use the education degree that I already have to make a living, and we believe God can provide in other ways too," we replied.

"This is very strange! What has happened to you?"

What indeed? Something wonderful had happened to Lorraine and me—something that changed our lives forever.

I had grown up like many other *Québécois* boys, going to our parish church with my parents each Sunday, even becoming an altar boy, serving with our priest from age nine until I was fourteen. I had learned on the street from age five that "the English" cause problems and are undesirable people. I became fiercely loyal to my friends, fighting on the streets of Montreal alongside the older boys against the gangs of *les Anglais* who lived in a nearby neighbourhood. Since I was little and very fast, I became the decoy who would creep up on them, pelt them with anything that was at hand, and then run for my life. Of course they would run after me, not knowing I was leading them right to the place where our gang was hiding. They had stones and slingshots ready to let our opponents have it. I didn't always make it there safely. I have scars on my body from those street enemies. Still, I was proud to show my peers what I could do.

This animosity was handed down from one generation to another even before the Conquest, when General Wolfe defeated General Montcalm at the battle for Quebec in 1759. England had been the enemy of our mother country, France, for many centuries, but it was when the New World was first discovered that they began to compete for supremacy outside of Europe. Both wanted the commerce and territorial rights in the newly discovered lands. England's Treaty of Paris with France in 1763 records that France surrendered our land and colony for two small islands near the coast of Newfoundland—St. Pierre and Miquelon.[4] That way she could retain her fishing rights to the rich aquatic harvest off the Grand Banks in the Atlantic.

Sold for several boatloads of fish! Betrayed by our mother France for two small islands! No wonder our forefathers had grown bitter. We thought England had taken everything from us, and we felt our mother country didn't care. We were now orphans, compelled to live in a home with foster parents who didn't even speak our language. Because we lost the land, we were forced to live under the rule of our enemy. We grew resentful, in a hurting blended family living alongside English and Natives.

After the Treaty of Paris (1763),[5] the more generous Quebec Act (1774) did allow the colonists to follow their Roman Catholic faith and to continue to speak French. The British even agreed to let the Church levy a parish tax, with which they could build stately churches and "sanctuaries" (shrines) to their favourite saints. This act sought to strengthen Britain's Quebec colony and cultivate peaceful relationships with its French inhabitants, a strategic step in view of the unrest in England's American colonies to the south.

To fulfill their part of the bargain, the priests took full responsibility for keeping their parishioners in submission to the British government and from joining the American Revolution by stressing the serious consequences of insurrection; one of them could be to lose what they had just acquired. They established small parishes that, they persuaded their people, would be family-style communities providing protection from danger and from evil outside influences. The clergy put together a school system, convincing their parishioners that a grade three education was sufficient for everyone, since they were peasants and would live all their lives on their farms, growing families. The Church would also protect them from the English and their cultish religion.

Since the *Québécois* fully trusted their religious leaders, they did not question their instructions. There was a spirit of unity and obedience in the parish, and few arguments arose. They all thought alike because they respected, even feared authority, at least on the surface. This tradition continued on, even until my parents' time. During the summer of 1955, I heard preaching that "French Canadians are born for little bread." I also witnessed the parishioners still assembled with their neighbours on the porch of Ste-Perpétue Church each Sunday after mass, where they knew there would be news and fellowship. It was there that all the problems of the parish (and indeed of the whole world) were resolved, and one could not miss that!

This traditional lifestyle formed the mindset of the French Canadian people. It fashioned our passions and character. It also cut us off from any chance of progress; our lack of business education and qualification for more profitable jobs deprived us of opportunities to become well-informed and prosperous.[6]

DONALD AND HIS AUNT PIERRETTE AVOINE ON THE PORCH OF
STE-PERPÉTUE CHURCH

Because of the long-standing traditions that had formed *Québécois* thinking, it wasn't surprising that our decision as a family to leave Quebec and study the Bible greatly alarmed some of our relatives. "What happened to make Donald and Lorraine change and turn from the ways of our fore-fathers and traditions? How can they be disloyal to our family's culture?"

But for us, something wonderful had happened.

## ATTEMPTS TO MAKE LIFE WORK...

The same attitude of hatred that had possessed me as a boy on the streets of Montreal followed me into my teens. Growing up did not change my life much, except that I stopped going to church following the winds of freedom of the 1970s. During my school years, I played baseball, hockey and football; I coached hockey and eventually owned a sports business. Lorraine, my wife and partner, was working many hours in the office, taking care of the administrative side of our business. Increased sales meant increased work. I neglected to spend holiday time with my children because I did not find the time; I was too busy and foolishly obsessed with building my own life to care about others. An unquenchable thirst to succeed consumed me. It almost ruined my marriage and family, but I couldn't stop climbing. Success was never enough. I wanted more and more; I was addicted. I was a blind workaholic trying to find fulfillment in the marketplace at any cost and at the expense of my loved ones. I became a difficult husband, a worse father and even a poor citizen.

Like me, Quebec was trying to find its identity—its *raison d'être*—and to build self-esteem through hockey. Our hockey idol, Maurice "the Rocket" Richard, opened this door for us.[7] Maurice himself suffered discrimination because he was French, but he persevered and became Canada's hockey icon. Quebec's sense of inequality increased. It felt short-changed by English Canada. For many *Québécois*, the only way to survive was to separate. I myself was convinced of this, so at age eighteen I joined the separatist *Parti Québécois*.

COACH DONALD WITH FAMOUS MAURICE "THE ROCKET" RICHARD, 1974

23

For all of my striving, life was beginning to crumble around me. In 1983, at the age of thirty-three, my existence seemed purposeless, insignificant. My pain came to a climax when a great community party was given to honour my "fifteen years of benevolent work in sports." Sprinkled throughout the sportsmen's "roast party," many flattering speeches and private compliments were showered upon me, but that night I hit the low point of my career. Ironically, I felt lost, unfulfilled, defeated, just like someone being ejected to retirement. Why such feelings? I was too young to deal with this!

"Is this all there is to life?" my mind kept asking. "Is there nothing more? Is life merely a dead end on a one-way street?" I had no answer. I experienced emptiness for the next three years. But in my empty existence a crossroad was graciously waiting for me.

I still remember March 20th, 1986, when something wonderful happened. Things began to change. I became more considerate of my wife, a better father to my children and a better citizen to my neighbours. Things became different, and our lives gained new meaning. That day something new came alive and started to penetrate and shape my life and family. Of course, my parents and other relations began to notice a transformation in our lives. "What has happened to Donald and Lorraine?" they asked one another. With our renewed spiritual beliefs, we didn't "fit into" the family as we once did. Were they thinking, as many others did, "From the beginning of our world here in Quebec, we have learned to live in one community, speak the same language, adopt one belief and practice the same religion. We have been united in that one spirit, we have had one set of moral standards and we followed one way of thinking. This has made life much easier for French Catholic people. How can those two now choose to be different?"

## CHALLENGING TRANSITION

This happened at a transitional time in Quebec when people around just remained silent when others walked away from church and faith, perhaps just preoccupied with seeing to their own things, seeking their personal enjoyment, and hardly knowing what to say or think about religious faith. Although today the Roman Catholic culture, if not faithfully practised, remains an important value among the 80 percent of *Québécois* (in 2000) who still consider themselves Roman Catholics, the great majority have dropped away from active involvement in the Church.[8] In this new reality, the clergy, for several centuries mostly all-powerful in the parishes, have been reduced to having cultural visibility but diminished authority. Who would have predicted such a revolution? Like a tsunami, freedom was sweeping across Quebec, and nothing could stop the flood of secularism. "Mind your own business" was the great new social commandment, and its corollary was "Enjoy yourself, as long as it feels good to you!"

When we experienced our faith renewal and demonstrated a sudden interest in the teaching of the Bible, what mattered to our family and friends was not that we feel better or be happier but that we continue to be in the family's evolving cultural space. All of a sudden, they were concerned that we had "changed our religion"; it bothered them. That was our fault—far greater than merely abandoning the practice of our family's traditional religion. We were now disloyal to our family's religion and, by extension, to its culture and traditions. Even though the 1960 Quiet Revolution was all about change and freedom, ironically the kind of change we were experiencing was not welcome at all. Later we learned how worried our relatives were about us.

DONALD WHEN HE WAS ALTAR BOY, WITH HIS SISTER JACYNTHE AT HER FIRST COMMUNION

You might take a *Québécois* out of the parish, but it's hard to take the parish out of a *Québécois'* mind. Has Quebec as a province become a kind of super-parish even today? Culture in Quebec is a dominant theme, and anything that is strange to the parish way is suspect. *Québécois* Catholics have been devoted religiously to the slogan "One language, one country and one religion."[9] These three entities have been Quebec's cultural jewels.[10] Historian Jean-Louis Lalonde writes that some stereotypical ideas were rooted in the collective memory of the Quebecois, such as: "French, therefore Catholic; English, therefore Protestant."[11]

Until 1993, French Protestants were still perceived by the Quebec Bishop's Assembly as people partaking in a cult;[12] in other words, they were people one must stay away from. Some of our relatives believed we had been caught up in some cult. After all, they knew that groups such as Protestants, Evangelicals, Jehovah's Witnesses and Mormons talk openly about God. Roman Catholics did not need to share their faith or to publicly talk about God; everyone was baptized as a baby and is safe in the Church. Our parents said one's belief is personal and private. To be French was to be Roman Catholic, and to be Roman Catholic was to belong to God. Why would Donald and Lorraine talk about God and study the Bible with English Protestants? After all, hadn't they learned that "outside Roman Catholic faith, there is no salvation" and "outside the parish, there is no security"? Something must be wrong! They must surely be suffering from depression or burnout!

To leave Montreal for Saskatchewan was a huge step for us and especially for our parents, who had never really travelled outside of Quebec. They suddenly became very protective and concerned about us.

## LITTLE FRENCH HOUSE ON THE PRAIRIE

We did not heed the warnings and advice that came from so many sides. So in August of 1988, we packed our U-Haul truck to leave for the West. My parents helped us, even though they did not agree with or understand what we were doing. After we departed, most communica-

HERE IS MY FAMILY WITH MY MOM AND DAD AS WE LEFT FOR SASKATCHEWAN

tion from Quebec stopped. We felt as if we had been placed on a black-list, effectively deleted from the French network. At the beginning, worried, like any caring parents would be, my mom and dad faithfully called on a monthly basis to get our news.

In spite of our family's incomprehension and fears, Briercrest Bible College in Saskatchewan was a wonderful institution and Caronport a suitable community in which our family would live, learn and be changed in our three marvellous years there. Caronport, on the Trans Canada Highway one hour west of Regina, was once an aviation base used by the Canadian Armed Forces during World War I. In 1935, the whole property was sold for one dollar to a group of Bible teachers from the nearby small town of Briercrest. From then on, Caronport was transformed into a spiritual base with the mission of training soldiers for Jesus Christ.

Our U-Haul truck and little family arrived there in August 1988, and on the morning of the 20th, we woke up to find ourselves in the middle of nowhere, surrounded by an ocean of wheat. Rather a change from the cosmopolitan city of Montreal! But as our forefathers from France had done along the St. Lawrence hundreds of years before, we proceeded to set

27

up our little French house in the centre of the western prairies. Though we didn't realize it, we were about to experience major culture shock.

CARONPORT, SK—SURROUNDED BY AN OCEAN OF WHEAT

### REFLECTING BACK ON EARLIER COLLEGE TIME IN QUEBEC (THE 1970S)

In Quebec colleges, teachers were allowed a great deal of freedom; they would never be rebuked for promoting nationalism in the classroom.[13] In the same way that priests taught and trained us to become Roman Catholics, teachers coached us to think like Quebec nationalists. Some would subtly instill feelings of guilt if one was not committed to a full buy-in to their cause. The class, responding with a certain "group-think," regarded as "cool" anyone who acted as a nationalist. Students showing any form of sympathy toward Canadian federalism were not affirmed; they were marginalized, often rejected. We students were crying out for freedom of speech in Canada! But what kind of freedom were we experiencing? Thus this thought pattern of intolerance and domination was passed from generation to generation.

I had taken the opportunity to learn basic English at school, so after getting my teacher's license at the University of Quebec in Montreal in 1973, I accepted the challenge of teaching French and physical education in an English elementary school in Greenfield Park, on the south shore of Montreal. This was during the 1970s, the era when the separatist nationalism of the *Front de Libération du Québec* (FLQ)[14] was at fever pitch and tension between the French and English was explosive. Perhaps subconsciously I was still fascinated by the struggle with *les Anglais* of Montreal! Or perhaps, as with other baby boomers who were entering the marketplace, I knew that functioning in English was the way to get ahead.

During that year, the grade six students would wait for me after class to provoke me and try to beat me up because I taught in French (as requested by the school) in my physical education classes. Every night I would come home exhausted. The situation seemed unbearable—too costly to my physical and mental health. I did not renew my contract, because the principal and parents were not willing to take proper actions to resolve that painful cultural clash. I left the school with even more bitterness toward the English.

During the Quiet Revolution, nationalist and separatist ideas were everywhere in the schools. The "truths" I accepted in the heat of peer pressure and classroom groupthink, combined with the personal negative experiences I had with the English, only fuelled my convictions and commitment to faith in Quebec nationalism. I came to believe that the only way for Quebec to survive was to separate from Canada. After the election of the *Parti Québécois* government in 1976, a new emphasis was placed on teaching Quebec history in the schools—and it was through a nationalist window.

## DISCOVERING THE WESTERN CANADIANS' WINDOW

While living in Saskatchewan, I was no longer seeking significance in Quebec culture and politics, or in sports. This was because a deep transformation had been working within me. From being a *gamin* (kid) who fought the English gangs on the streets of Montreal a few years earlier to now living totally among English-speaking people to whom French culture meant little—well, it was a major change! Here I was—not long ago a separatist—living with my family in Western Canada, surrounded by my former "enemies."

29

My wife, Lorraine, and I could speak just enough of the language to communicate about the simple things of everyday life. Our low proficiency in English was a huge disadvantage. Not only did we relish the opportunity to improve ourselves through acquiring English, but as parents we were happy that our children, Martin and Claudiane,[15] would now add a new language and culture to their heritage that would benefit them in the future. We hadn't been in Caronport long, however, before I discovered that English and French Canadians were looking at our country through two different windows. Many people whom we met in our three years in the West believed that the *Québécois* were never satisfied. No wonder that in any negotiation by Quebec a spirit of mutual mistrust would prevail and harm the process. Had Quebec become expert at using his bargaining power to demand and protect his rights? In the West, people thought so.

They were less knowledgeable about our longstanding fears. The *Québécois* were convinced that they had been abused, mistreated and misunderstood by the English. We had a lot of cultural self-esteem to recover after the humiliation of the 1759 Conquest, and we felt the English were not interested in giving it back. We believed they thought like Lord Durham, a well-known British governor who strongly recommended in 1840 that English Canada assimilate us culturally, thus solving Canada's ethnic problem once and for all. "It would be for their good," he had opined, thinking he had solved the issue. "It would deliver them from their inferiority complex." Understandably, his comment enraged the people of Quebec.

During our first year in Saskatchewan, we were invited to classes, schools and churches to give our story. People were curious to hear our testimonies about why we (*Québécois*) had chosen to study in Western Canada, but we soon found out they were hesitant to discuss politics. Several cautiously warned me not to mention the political situation. Some said, "This subject is very explosive; it's a time bomb!"

Even though the area of public relations was my strength, I was not the kind of person who longs to be "politically correct" at any cost. While I could keep from initiating a discussion about Quebec, I never avoided an open door to share our side of the story. We knew that our new friends had a different understanding of the subject; just from watching the news in Western Canada, we saw a different point of view. English TV news, opinion pieces and editorials presented a drastically different perspective than those from French Quebec. Sometimes as I spoke about Quebec and Canada, I sensed people were getting nervous, and I often wondered why. But we also felt that we were led into something very special.

## RUDE CONFRONTATION

The climax came one day on campus. I was walking toward the bookstore when I met another student. Nodding to him, I said in my strong French accent, "Allo! How are you doing?"

He stopped suddenly, looked me in the face and, pointing his finger at me, replied, "What's wrong with you *Québécois?*"

Not too long before that, I would never have tolerated a finger in my face. My background was sports, where I learned to compete; a winner never lets his opponent intimidate or attack him. "Never drop your eyes and show him you are intimidated!"—this was the way we successful coaches trained winning hockey players in Quebec. Now you can imagine how I felt! Immediately I was on my toes, looking at him eyeball to eyeball, ready to resist his attack. After all, I am *Québécois!* I have Latin blood in me. *Should I let him have it? What does he know about Quebec?* But also I was a spiritually renewed believer, and deep inside my heart I knew I needed to act differently.

The student started to vent his aversion to Quebec. It was like unloading a garbage truck on me. I had never experienced such humiliation. What was happening? Wasn't this a Bible college? After travelling over 3,000 kilometres, I thought I had come to paradise, surrounded by Christians. I hadn't expected this! Soon, I realized that I was not in heaven, not yet.

Immediately something amazing happened inside me. The more I listened, the more I started to sense my opponent's hurts and feel his pain. As I listened, suddenly I realized that English Canadians were also feeling rejection and insecurity. Quebec wanted to leave Canada, making her a fragmented nation; the *Québécois* usually seemed unhappy with the federal government and the rest of the provinces. Quebec had enjoyed the 1967 World's Fair, the Montreal Canadiens hockey club was breaking NHL records for Stanley Cup wins, the 1976 Olympic games were in Montreal— Quebec was benefiting from a lot of federal spending and national prominence yet still demanded more money and autonomy or he would walk away from the confederation other Canadians cherished so much.

Suddenly, I found myself listening carefully to him. The more he talked, the more my eyes were opened to see through his window. Before this I would have said, "You English deserve it for all the pain you have inflicted on us through the centuries!" But now I was feeling his pain, the pain of an English-heritage man. When he finished unloading his anger on me, I looked at him and said, "For the wounds, the hurts, the pain we have caused you, would you forgive us?"

Unexpectedly, he broke into tears—and, stunned, I did also. This was a new experience for both of us; it was the pathway to reconciliation. We were experiencing a very unique moment. This gave us an opportunity to talk about the French-English relationship empathetically, and we shared both the Western and *Québécois'* viewpoints calmly from our respective windows.

I began to understand that I might have my convictions about the French, Native and English Canadian relationships but I definitely did not have a monopoly on the truth. I could speak only from the perspective I had experienced growing up. This moment was crucial for my personal spiritual growth and relationships. That day we both set out on a path toward reconciliation and the peace and joy that it can bring. What a lesson! Not only did we discover each other's personal window, we also needed to look at the matter from another point of view—through the window of reconciliation.

### TRAINING IN COUNSELLING

After two years of Bible studies, I was ready to enter the family counselling program. The things I had been anticipating to learn in family counselling resonated strongly with the deep changes in my life that had climaxed on that watershed day, March 20, 1986. I was not disappointed. From the beginning, the knowledge and skills really impacted our life as a family at the growing edge.

People who are in a crisis consult counsellors in order to resolve a particular problem from the past or to learn how to deal with a disturbing challenge that has come up. Rarely will they go for preventive instruction; instead they go when they are experiencing turmoil and stress—in other words, when it really hurts. "Please take away my pain!" or "Please give me a quick fix!" is their plea.

MARTIN — DONALD — CLAUDIANE — LORRAINE PHOTO AFTER 1991
GRADUATION

In our courses, we learned that a counsellor needs to be compassionate. We were trained to identify the crisis and recognize that the hurts and problems are an outward expression of deep internal wounds. Hurting at the core of their being, the counsellor's clients usually respond with self-protection by building walls around themselves. Sometimes there are healthy responses; at other times, negative reactions. Like a mirror, their behaviour and felt emotions reflect what is going on inside their minds and hearts. Whenever people experience pain, their inadequacy to deal with it is exposed; unfortunately most of the time pride and self-pity override their need to get help. This eventually develops into a lifestyle that is difficult to change. Our role is to help them see, understand, be transformed and learn to walk in victorious ways.

We also learned that counsellors are not there to judge people or their emotions or behaviour. After all, we all know how painful a broken relationship can be. That is why in our biblical studies we learned about the need for reconciliation. But this concept is foreign to human nature. Rather, people who are hurt seek to control other people or circumstances as a measure of self-protection. They may indulge in self-pity or vengeance in their attempt to make life work. Could this explain why the major cultural groups in Canada hold on to past grievances and so create friction when they encounter each other? We also learned that unresolved conflicts and broken relationships can create tragic relational time bombs and multiple hurts.

From all the teaching we got, one idea caught our attention: both our spiritual-cultural and genetic heritages are handed down from our parents. They pass on to their children the very behavioural characteristics they inherited. I can easily see some of my own personality traits, manners, habits and attitudes in my children, and no doubt my parents could see theirs in me.

The best way to deal with an unhealthy behaviour is to discover its root causes. Using a similar approach, a doctor may say to his client, "You need surgery in order to get at the root of the pain and illness you are experiencing, and when we cut it out you should feel fine again." Our teacher said, "Get to know the background of your client and you will be amazed how much it facilitates you to help him move forward in life."

Something similar to this always remained in the back of my mind. My friend Harold Lutzer,[16] director of Canadian Revival Fellowship, enjoyed talking with me about Quebec. Each time I met with him, he would ask me questions about our politics or any subject that would help him better understand the *Québécois* and their religious culture. Harold never gave up encouraging me to publish this story of Quebec, the grown-up orphan, and the account of our personal journey to Reconciliation through the Canadian hurting blended family.

Our training in family counselling has equipped us to help free individuals from the pain of broken relationships. It also helped us to understand the Quebec-Canada controversies and the hurting relationships among Native, French, and English people. The portrait of Quebec I made in class one day as a case study led to writing this allegory. Quebec's story cast as a counselling scenario became not only an authentic, interesting case study but also a revealing venture.

❧ ————————————————

4      There were other aspects to the Treaty of Paris, as it settled a more extensive war with European and seagoing action.

5      The Treaty of Paris (1763) was an agreement between France and England after the English conquered New France in North America, and from there the French had to live with Native and English to form Canada.

6      Michel Brunet, "The British Conquest and the Canadiens." Essay featured in *Approaches to Canadian History*, p. 9. The low standard of education in French Canada was one of the numerous misfortunes that befell the *Canadiens* after the Conquest of their homeland.

7      I encourage you to watch *The Rocket* (Cinémaginaire Inc., 2005), which tells the story of hockey player Maurice Richard and portrays the tensions between English and French in the National Hockey League. (For example, referees frequently discriminated against Maurice, Quebec's hero.)

8      Lemieux and Montminy, *Le catholicisme Québécois*, p. 8.

9      R.P. Duclos, *Histoire du protestantisme français au Canada et aux États-Unis*, pp. 12-13.

10      Lemieux and Montminy, *Le catholicisme Québécois*, p. 17. For Lemieux and Montminy, the Catholic religion is not only a part of the *Québécois* culture, it is also the cultural matrix. We cannot talk about *Québécois* culture without talking about Catholicism and its huge influence in shaping the life of its people. It is the historical bedrock of Quebec.

11    Lalonde, *Des loups dans la bergerie*, p. 13. This was hardly surprising, considering the stereotypes about French and Catholic, English and Protestant embedded in everyone's minds.

12    Richard Lougheed, Wesley Peach and Glen Smith, *Histoire du protestantisme au Québec depuis 1960: une analyse anthropologique, culturelle et historique*, p. 9.

13    I attended *CEGEP Rosemont* in Montreal from 1968-70. *CEGEP* is a sort of junior college that is unique to the Quebec educational system.

14    The *Front de Libération du Québec* "Front of Quebec Liberation" was a clandestine group that supported the Quebec sovereignty movement through acts of terrorism.

15    Martin was ten and Claudiane eight, a good age to learn English in an immersion context.

16    Harold Lutzer, my mentor, is a farmer and executive director of Canadian Revival Fellowship, an organization that teaches and trains in spiritual renewal.

# CHAPTER 1

# COUNSELLING IN PROGRESS: "JE ME SOUVIENS..."

## WHAT'S THE MATTER?

❧

*[Quebec (Qc) is meeting with a counsellor (Cr).]*

*[Counselling in progress...]*

Cr: Hello! Welcome.

Qc: Thank you.

Cr: What can I do for you?

Qc: I have been referred to you by a friend.

Cr: A friend?

Qc: Yes, my friend Donald said you were the right person to help me.

Cr: Good to hear from Donald. Yes, I know him well. How can I help you today?

Qc: I told Donald I need to talk to someone. I need help to understand myself. How is this going to happen?

Cr: Today, I will ask you to give me a general overview of what you have on your mind. After that, we will talk about how the sessions might go, and then we can work from there. How about that?

Qc: It looks like a good plan.

Cr: Let us start. What would you like me to know about you?

Qc: For a while I have been struggling—feeling as though I am going nowhere in life. There are times I feel empty. Other times I wrestle with who I am. Sometimes I feel a red hot volcano smoking inside of me. I wonder why. I love partying! This is where I have fun—and forget and relax!

[*The counsellor actively observes, while Quebec's eyes are glued to the window as if searching for something—a new insight, another perspective, a longing for a fresh understanding of some sort.*]

Cr: Can you explain to me what you mean when you say that sometimes you feel like you are "going nowhere in life"? Can you give me an example?

Qc: I am a driven person; I love to be involved; I have lots of energy; this I know. I am proud of whom I am, but somehow I feel empty—that life is futile, that I don't fit. I'm confused, feeling I'm being pulled in two directions. There is no secure nest where I can lie down and relax. What is life about?

Cr: How long has this been going on?

Qc: It's been like that since I was a young adult. [*Pauses, then continues with emotion.*] I feel like one who has been playing forever in someone else's backyard or living in another person's home. Now that I am an adult, there is a feeling in my heart that it's time to find out who I am, to find out where I belong.

Cr: Don't you have a family?

Qc: [*Quebec looks at the window once more.*] Where I live, I feel the other children want me to be like them. But I am different, I am distinct...Even though I keep repeating it, they don't understand. I have my own identity. Maybe I have a language barrier....

Cr: Language barrier? Don't you speak the same language in your family?

Qc: In my foster home, we speak many languages since we come from different backgrounds. [*Thoughtful pause.*] Sometimes part of me wants to separate from my so-called "family." Then another part of me wants to stay around—to belong. Yes, to belong! Why is that? It's confusing and stressing me out....

Cr: You just mentioned "foster home" and "so-called family"?

Qc: [*Quickly replies.*] You bet! I do not really have a family. Maybe it's some sort of blended family. Do you know what I mean?

Cr: I know what a foster home is and a blended family, yes. Tell me more about that.

Qc: After we (French Canadians) were conquered by the British in 1759, we were forced to live with a bunch of English-speaking people whom we did not choose at all. So for us, it's not family! It's just...hmm...to be polite...[*Searching for words, Quebec looks at the counsellor for help.*]

Cr: Feel free here. Use the words you think are the most appropriate. This will help me understand better how you see and feel things.

Qc: Thank you!...It's not a family...it's a gang, an *English gang*. Or, if you like, I would say it's an English *foster home*. It's filled with English who are now the real children in this place.

Cr: Real children?

Qc: Yes, real children, meaning legitimate. They let us know *they* are the children of the conqueror...and that we are just the kids who are *the ones conquered*...I feel like an orphan. The way they relate to us makes us feel they are the ones who call the shots for the Canadian family and that we are second-rate people. [*The counsellor can observe bitterness in Quebec's expression.*]

Cr: Why do you see yourself an orphan? Did you lose your parents?

Qc: [*Hesitant to answer.*] Yes and no. Not really...yes, really! Anyway, life worked out in such a way that we are now in this English foster home.

Cr: Then how is the orphan notion fitting in here if your parents are still living?

Qc: They kind of abandoned us. It's a long story...let's just call it a tragedy; it's too long to talk about today! [*Quebec resists getting into this subject here.*]

Cr: Hmm. Are there any other children? How do they cope in the family?

Qc: Yes, there are others. But it is not a family! People want to make us believe we are a family—the English worked hard at changing the native kids' names to English ones to sound more "civilized" and more "Canadian." They did not try this scheme with us French kids, though, or with most of the new foreigners. That word *family* is pure illusion—more than that, it is a lie. We never did live as a family. We French never have belonged, never been welcome. There have been constant tension and battles between us since our arrival in America and even long before that, in Europe, which proves we will never understand each other!

Cr: You are saying ongoing battles, right?

Qc: *Oui*! This is how it goes. Since we came together under Canada as a blended family, each time that we have fought over issues seeking for a solution it seems there is always a winner and a loser in the final tally. As a result, someone is satisfied; the other is unhappy. Any gain we make always ends up being used as a weapon against us until the next crisis. No matter what verbal or written agreements we make, they never satisfy anyone for very long. It's obvious. And it's never enough. Battles keep coming back. That's the Canadian reality.

Cr: Do these battles include all the children?

Qc: *Oh yes*! Every group of blended children seems to be unhappy with each other. No rest! When you think you have a peaceful moment in the home, another crisis gets started through an issue with a group.

Cr: This Canadian family life seems a tricky challenge, then? And this seems to worry you?

Qc: Yes! Very much! We have a history of unresolved broken relationships.

Cr: Why do you say this?

Qc: Because problems and crises and demands are coming back over and over....

Cr: It seems to be a big weight on your mind.

Qc: It's messy...In this pitiful "family," we constantly feel as if we're dealing with angry people and fighting over everything. Relating to each other is like walking on eggs...broken eggs would be more appropriate. You've got to watch yourself all the time! Did you know our family life is always before the courts? Lawsuits have become commonplace, with one or another group of us making money at the expense of the other children! It seems to be *the way*.

Cr: I sense you have a different opinion or feeling on this question. Don't you?

Qc: This way of interacting has nothing to do with family living! We are far away from the family values I have known before in the parish of my youth. Is it worth living here?

Cr: So what's on your mind?

Qc: This is the tension I'll talk to you about: sometimes I feel like staying in the family, and some days I'd rather separate; it never seems to be resolved...Anyway, I just wanted to meet with you today. I did not expect to go through a long session. As I said, I came to see if you can help me.

Cr: [*Looking into Quebec's eyes to communicate empathy.*] Thank you for sharing. I am pleased to be involved in your life, and I will do my best. Now, let me explain how I intend to work with you.

Qc: Thank you! Go ahead.

Cr: Between sessions of counselling, I will ask you to prepare by doing a bit of homework.

Qc: Homework? That was not my strength at school!

Cr: What I am going to ask you to do will help you to understand what is going on in your mind. Sometimes, when we concentrate too much on a painful experience, we lose sight of life. In the light of your life story, we will look for some key insights and answers for you. If you feel comfortable with this and with me, we can go ahead.

Qc: You make me feel comfortable. Okay, I can give homework a try!

Cr: For our next meeting, I want you to take a look back at your family roots, your childhood and your life in Europe before you came to live in America as New France.

Qc: How can I do this?

Cr: As you concentrate on your childhood in Europe, you can refer back to your own memories, do some reading of history, talk to other French *Québécois* and reflect on how life was for you then. You can talk to your friend Donald as well. Talk to him about his particular perspective on Quebec history; his insights might help you understand some of the questions you have.

Qc: Okay. I know Donald has a special perspective on Canadian history; he speaks across Canada on broken relationships among French, Native and English, reconciliation and healing.

Cr: Well, I know this work will demand significant effort from you, but I feel it is worth doing. Finally, take notes whenever an insight touches you in the process of reading and discussing. Some people like to do journaling; it might help as well. Bring your journal and notes to our meetings.

Qc: I did not know counselling would make me work like this!

Cr: There are different ways to do this. We've had a good start. I hope you will see life making more sense.

Qc: That would be nice! *Oui*, I'll give it a try.

Chapter 2

# Historical Insights
## Life in France before 1600

### A Race to Discover the New World

Until the end of the 16th century, several nations were in a race to expand into the New World. France, Portugal, Spain (all Roman Catholic countries) and England were in hostile competition with each other, driven to gain power and control, fighting for territorial, commercial, material and financial interests. Spain and Portugal's desires lay mainly in Central and South America and the southern part of the present USA. France and England were focused on the north. While searching to find a sea route to Asia in order to get access to its resources, they discovered America. The English got into the race by denying and challenging the papal decrees as well as by global ambition. Economic opportunities motivated them to invest in establishing colonies and business in America. The fur trade's lucrative commercial potential pushed France and England into further military and religious struggle.

### Discovery of America

Who discovered America? The aboriginal (Indian and Inuit) people first occupied the land, while the Vikings, like Eric the Red, left their mark on its soil as far back as the tenth century. Spain and Portugal were struggling for supremacy in the same area, so they asked the pope, who had much influence in European affairs at the time, to resolve their differences by granting exclusive jurisdiction in areas of the New World they explored.

In his attempt to keep his Church's children from fighting, Pope Alexander VI issued a papal bull in 1493 granting present-day Brazil to Portugal and the other lands to Spain. The bull also decreed that any person who would disobey this order would risk excommunication from the Roman Catholic Church.[19] Having a powerful influence on the world, the pope established a monopoly for just two Roman Catholic countries, which seemed unfair for the other countries professing to be part of the same religious family.

In 1501, Gaspar Corte-Real went from Portugal to America. In 1520, Portugal, through Joao Alvares Fafundes, attempted to establish the first North American colony. Portugal's navigators made vital contributions to the development of the science of mapping (cartography). After this effort, Portugal invested more resources into fishing.

Spain's amazing discoveries were concentrated in South America: gold, silver, pearls and expensive wood helped Spain become the richest country in Europe. In 1503, they discovered Florida. In 1521, they conquered Mexico to establish New Spain. But Spain and Portugal were not the main competitors with France in America. England was.

## ENGLAND CHALLENGES PAPAL AUTHORITY

Even though England's King Henry VII (1485-1509) acknowledged Rome's religious authority, he rejected the 1493 papal bull. Henry claimed the right to his share of the New World, and England jumped into the race.[20] He put together a partnership with John Cabot, an Italian living in England at the time, and equipped him to go and discover new territory. Cabot landed on Canada's shore in 1497 and claimed America for England. The success of this trip provided a solid foundation for England's claim on America.

When England removed its churches from papal oversight, with King Henry VIII (1509-1547) becoming the head of the English church hierarchy, the country felt full freedom to claim and conquer the New World. In 1527, Henry sent another ship to the New World under John Rut's command. Rut visited Cape Breton Island, entered the Gulf of

Hochelaga (St. Lawrence today) and sailed along the coast of present-day New England. His expedition served as the basis for England's claim to the land that became the American colonies.[21] At the end of the sixteenth century, England, now spiritually served by the essentially Protestant Church of England, was at war with powerful Roman Catholic France.

## FRANCE WAS LOOKING FOR THE POPE'S BLESSING

During that period, France was growing in ascendancy and wanted a good share of New World spoils. How could their country avoid the pope's excommunication and still gain the resources of the New World? François I devised a clever plan. He decided to claim that France's expeditions were only for missionary purposes rather than for gaining new land and commercial wealth. A new pope, Clement VII, helped the situation by reinterpreting the 1493 papal bull as applying to past discoveries only. In 1533, François I and Clement VII met to arrange a new deal, opening the door for France's king to claim French rights to the New World.

The first French expedition was sent out in 1524. A group of Italians, working for France, organized an expedition headed by Giovanni da Verrazano and sent him westward to find Asia. His discoveries prompted France to claim its rights in America. The French gave the name "New France" to the land that stretches from Florida to Cape Breton Island; Roman Catholic Cardinal Richelieu of France still claimed this territory in 1627 in the name of his country.[22]

In 1534, François I financed Jacques Cartier and sent him to explore the New World. His ship stopped at Cape Bonavista in Newfoundland, explored the gulf and went up the great Hochelaga (St. Lawrence) River for many miles. He was one of many who discovered America. He stopped at Pointe-de-Quenouille (Gaspé today) and planted a cross, which bore the fleur-de-lis and the words *"Vive le Roi de France"* (long live the king of France). It was "a fitting symbol of the close relationship between church and state in the New France thus claimed," reported historian Mason Wade.[23] This revealed France's hidden vision for America. Even though Jacques Cartier's journal noted that he prayed with Indians to thank God for discovering the land, according to Wade he merely paid lip service to the professed missionary motives.[24] France was in America to do serious business with the fur trade.

A REPLICA OF THE CROSS ERECTED BY JACQUES CARTIER, 1563, JULY 24TH

Ever since the pope's unfair apportionment of the new lands (New World) between Spain and Portugal, there was scarcely any means for France to intervene without risking a religious war, other than to take on a missionary role herself. That this role was only a diplomatic facade is evident when we realize that the first baptism in New France took place almost 100 years later (1610).[25] Wade supports this:

> Missionary activity was not the primary purpose of the French coming to America, despite the claims of most French-Canadian writers. New France was frequented by explorers and traders for nearly a century before the first missionaries came.[26]

The first mission station acknowledged was Ville-Marie (Montreal) in 1642.

> When the French merchants fixed their [sights] on North America, their vision revealed not souls, but business potential...The fur

46

trade remained the mainspring of the colony's life [and] Jacques Cartier and his French partners' primary aims were exploration [and] the discovery of treasures and business potential.[27]

The long religious wars in Europe were leaving their fingerprints; they were all about a battle for political power and control over earthly things and kingdoms.

## RELIGIOUS INTOLERANCE IN FRANCE

Back in France, the king and his cardinals were experiencing other problems apart from their wars with England. The Protestant Reformation in the early 1500s produced other reformers besides Martin Luther. In Paris, a young Frenchman by the name of Jean Calvin taught biblical themes that were contrary to Roman Catholic doctrines. Because of his teaching, Calvin was put on blacklist by the Church and he was forced to flee. He joined the Genevan Church in Switzerland, where he became the major theologian.

His friends in France joined the "Calvinists" and eventually became known as "Huguenots," probably after a Swiss spiritual leader named Besançon Hugues. They were skilled, industrious people and prospered greatly, especially in southeastern France around the city of La Rochelle. There they established a political stronghold—a "state within a state," including cities of their own. Besides being skilled artisans, these people were also expert sailors. They had the reputation of being favoured by God everywhere they lived. It was reported that when Jacques Cartier sailed up the Gulf of Hochelaga, believing he had discovered this great body of water, he found fishing vessels from La Rochelle there ahead of him. This was the famed fishing paradise favoured by several European countries.

Huguenots increased in economic and social influence in France.[28] A number of noblemen joined their group, including Henry, King of Navarre, and Admiral Gaspard de Coligny, who became their leader. This burst of expansion so greatly alarmed the French court that persecution broke out against them. Initially, these Protestants continued to flourish, which in turn attracted more persecution, until life in France became almost unbearable for them. From 1562, France practiced religious intolerance toward Huguenots; it ceased to be a land of freedom in the survivors' minds.[29]

This was in the high period of the Reformation, when theological controversy and wars of religion racked the great nations of Europe. Bloody religious strife was carried across the sea from the Old World to New Spain, New France, and New England.[30]

Was there a place in the New World where they could enjoy freedom of life and conscience? Motivated to find a refuge for French believers who were persecuted in France, Coligny, the Huguenots' leader, sent Jean Ribault and Goulaine de Laudonnière to America.

A previous effort to start a colony had been made earlier under Roberval, who was designated lieutenant–general of the king in the New World. While Roberval was detained in Europe, his subordinate, Jacques Cartier, set off in the spring of 1541, stayed in America for the winter and sailed back to France, wrongly thinking he had found gold. Roberval arrived in America in 1542, but his efforts to start a colony were in vain.

Ribault and de Laudonnière founded a first New France, which was maintained until 1564.[31] The Spanish tried hard to fight any Protestants. Menendez massacred Ribault's French Protestants in Florida in an effort to destroy and ruin the first New France, but France never managed to fight off these Catholic Spanish attackers. In all fairness, it must be noted that the English Puritans were barring Roman Catholics from their New England colony while the Roman Catholics were attempting to eliminate Huguenots from America. European religious intolerance left its marks on the birth and development of the American colonies.

After Coligny, there would not be another intentional effort to develop a New France colony until the seventeenth century. The "first" New France was practically forgotten by France, who was busy fighting about religion in her European backyard.[32]

In August 1572, the Massacre of St. Barthélemy took place, in which numerous thousands of Huguenots[33] were killed, including their leader, Coligny. Atrocious persecution motivated hundreds of thousands of Huguenots to flee to England, Germany, Switzerland and other European countries;[34] eventually still others took advantage of openings to sail to North America, where they hoped to establish a settlement that would provide them with security along with some religious and economic freedom.

Then, under Henri IV of France, a period of religious tolerance prevailed as in 1598 he passed the Edict of Nantes, granting freedom of religion in France. Henri IV, who had been ruler of a little kingdom called Navarre, had Calvinist roots. His mother, Jeanne III, commonly known as Jeanne d'Albret, had become a Protestant in 1560.[35] In 1561, she signed an authorization for Calvinism. She became so highly committed to spread these doctrines throughout France that by 1568 she was leading the Protestants of La Rochelle. At the death of King François II in 1560, Henri's Roman Catholic father took him to the French court to learn about Roman Catholicism and get closer to the decision makers. Later, Jeanne III negotiated with Paris a strategic position for her son through a wedding with Marguerite de France in 1572; she would remain Roman Catholic, to Jeanne's great regret, but it was a religious compromise to assure Henri's future. To complete his parents' scheme, Henri became a Roman Catholic, a requirement to become king of France.

Henri IV's edict allowed freedom of religion, stopped the persecution and opened the way for several French expeditions to New France with Huguenots on board.[36] The New World was a "dream country" for them. There they hoped to build their safe, hopeful nests. Huguenots were gifted navigators, remarkable chiefs of expedition and skilled sailors who could ensure success for the French expeditions. Henri IV backed gifted Huguenot entrepreneurs like Pierre Du Gua de Mons, who formed a friendship with him in La Rochelle. Several Huguenot businessmen participated in the fur trade and the colonization of New France.

On numerous expeditions, Roman Catholic priests and Protestant ministers sailed on the same ship. At times, Roman Catholics strongly complained about the Huguenots singing hymns and biblical psalms while at sea.[37] These brought back painful memories of the former time when Huguenots were persecuted and murdered by Roman Catholics. Though both parties were required to coexist aboard a ship led by French Huguenot navigators, relationships were generally inharmonious.

King Henri's assassination in Paris in 1610 was bad news for Huguenots. Persecution and terrorism resumed under the leadership of France's highest Roman Catholic authority, Cardinal Richelieu; he developed a strategy for strengthening the French monarchy, imposing one religion and one language under one great nation with the support of the new king, Louis XIII.

"Heresy must be eliminated at all cost!" claimed Richelieu, who directed a new war against the Huguenots. Was this a religious or a political attempt? His perception was that the great city of La Rochelle was a nation within the nation of France; he captured their great fortress and other key cities and harassed the Huguenots until their political power disintegrated. It is estimated that La Rochelle, a city of 25,000, was reduced to 5,000 in 1628, much of the population having died from siege-induced starvation. England tried to help by sending soldiers to Ré Island, but their initiative miserably failed. "What are the English doing again in our family business?" was the natural question on France's part. This became one more offence the French would hold against the English. "*Je me souviens...*" (I do remember...) captures French sentiment on such interference, no matter how humanitarian its motive may have been.

After Louis XIV came to the throne, he repealed the Edict of Nantes in 1685 and persecution became relentless. Under Jesuit influence, harsh means were used to induce France's Protestants to join the Roman Catholic Church. Parents were forced to have their newborn babies baptized into "the one true Roman Church" or risk having them sent to convents and brought up as Roman Catholics. Richelieu created the "Dragonets," an evil system in which soldiers were permitted to take any appropriate action to convert Protestants.[38] These included child abduction, brutality, rape, arson and murder.[39] Cardinal Richelieu's strategy had been successfully imposed on France.

This declaration of war and its bloody mass murders and terrorism caused the Protestant countries professing Calvinist faith to mobilize against France. Holland, Prussia, Scotland and England had one faith to protect and one enemy in common; they were determined and united in fighting France, their haughty neighbour.

50

The emigration of the prosperous Huguenot refugees was dramatically increasing. Those who survived fled to France's enemies, as others had about forty years earlier, taking their treasures and industrial know-how with them. They strengthened England's economy and military might. Serious consequences against France would emerge, and there would be a long battle between England and France for the American colonies.

This emigration was a disastrous loss to the country. Authors and historians have associated the growth of capitalism in France with the development of Bible-focused Reformation groups[40] France's economy was bleeding so considerably that, in 1685, the Court of Louis XIV issued a proclamation forbidding any more Protestants to leave the French borders with the threat of losing their lives or being used as slaves on French ships. Still 150,000 to 200,000 successfully fled France between 1680 and 1700.[41] Apparently Richelieu's policy of "one nation, one language, and one religion" eventually weakened rather than united France, while strategically serving her rivals in their quest for the New World.

## FOUNDATIONS REALLY MATTER

Each nation involved in the race for the New World laid exclusive claim to the territories it explored and wanted, establishing colonies to develop and monopolize the lucrative business of fur. Because of this, the First Nations people were trapped in this "run for your life" competition, trying to protect their land and culture and to survive against two aggressive colonizers, France and England.

And the Huguenot colonists continued to be targets of France (and allies of Reformed England). Lalonde writes,

> The battle between Catholics and Huguenots and Protestants fills the memory of all when France is attempting to establish a permanent colony at the end of the XVI century.[42]

The Huguenots played a significant though underestimated role in the early establishing of the French colony in the New World.[43] Like the First Nations people, they became victims of the religious aspect of the European competition for North America.

51

The age-old European struggle between French and English, their fight for the business of furs and America's land mass, their strategy of controlling and enslaving the Indians and their wars of religion led to harsh racial, national and religious rivalry and militarism. These dynamics helped shape the troubled foundations on which French, Native and English people would relate to one another in North America on a long-term basis.

Through this early window on our history, which reveals such rivalry and conflict at the outset, we understand that Canada was built on competitive relationships among these three main founding nations. Even today, the shocking reality is that this heritage lives on, having been transmitted from one generation to another. Our national fathers' main priority was to build and develop the commercial fur trade by almost any profitable means, but Europe's spiritual and nationalistic struggles took root with the commerce. The lesson we learn is that the basic foundations on which a country is built really matter in order to define its future.

�֎ ———————————————

[19]    Jacques Lacoursière, *Histoire populaire du Québec: des origines à 1791*, Tome I, p.13.

[20]    Marcel Trudel, *Initiation à la Nouvelle France*, p.9.

[21]    Ibid., 10.

[22]    Trudel, *Initiation*, p. 15. The original New France, established by Verrazano in 1524, spanned all of North America.

[23]    Wade, *French Canadians*, p. 7.

[24]    Ibid., p. 4.

[25]    Trudel, *Initiation*, p. 19.

[26]    Wade, *French Canadians*, p.4.

[27]    Ibid.

[28]    Bosher had done extensive studies showing the positive influence of Protestantism on capitalism.

29    Michel Gaudette, *Guerre des religions d'ici*, p. 13.

30    Wade, *French Canadians*, p. 2.

31    Trudel, *Initiation*, p.22.

32    Ibid.

33    "St. Bartholomew's Day massacre," http://en.wikipedia.org/wiki/ St._Bartholomew%E2%80%99s_Day_Massacre. From August to October, similar apparently spontaneous massacres of Huguenots took place in other towns, such as Toulouse, Bordeaux, Lyon, Bourges, Rouen, and Orléans. Some recent historian researchers estimate the number of dead at 2,000 in Paris and 5,000 to 10,000 in the rest of France.

34    Lalonde, *Des loups dans la bergerie*, p. 18.

35    *"Henri IV de France,"* http://fr.wikipedia.org/wiki/Henri_IV_ de_France.

36    Lalonde, *Des loups dans la bergerie*, p. 28.

37    Ibid.

38    Robert Larin, *Brève Histoire des protestants en Nouvelle-France et au Québec* (XVIe-XIXe siècles), p. 45.

39    Lalonde, *Des loups dans la bergerie*, p. 32.

40    Gaudette, *Guerres de religions*, p. 12.

41    Robert Larin, *Brève Histoire des protestants en Nouvelle-France et au Québec* (XVIe—XIXe siècles), p. 47.

42    Lalonde, *Des loups dans la bergerie*, p. 18.

43    Larin, *Brève histoire*, p. 31.

# CHAPTER 3

# "JE ME SOUVIENS..."

## OPENING A WINDOW ON QUEBEC'S CHILDHOOD IN FRANCE

❧

*[Counselling in progress...]*

Cr: Last time we met, I asked you to prepare to talk about your family roots and your childhood. How did your homework go?

Qc: It's okay. Reading brought back good memories of family life.

Cr: Tell me, how was life in Europe?

Qc: France was our "Mother country." We were a growing family, the biggest in the European neighbourhood. Professing Roman Catholicism, Mom was called *la fille aînée de Rome* (the elder daughter of Rome) because of her strong involvement in the Church and faithful commitment to the pope.[44] This attribute was something our parents were exceptionally proud of, and it affirmed our belief in the Roman Church. Mother was also dreaming about material prosperity and preoccupied by the way she could ensure the best future for the family. I once heard Mom say that the family dream was to control the world's business. A bright future was before us.

Cr: How was life in the neighbourhood?

Qc: We fought Portugal and Spain, neighbours who wanted the same thing. But all being Catholic, our parents worked hard to be "politically correct" in relating with them.

Cr: You talked about Spain and Portugal. Was there any other neighbour?

Qc: Of course there were the English!

55

Cr: What about them? It sounds as if you were not too close to them.

Qc: As a matter of fact, they are the ones who were too close to us—

Cr: Sorry to interrupt; why do you say *too close*?

Qc: Well, though they lived in England, they occupied part of our French backyard and field...Most Canadians don't know that the French and English did not learn to fight each other in Canada. Did you know that?

Cr: That's interesting! Tell me more about it.

Qc: Rivalry and fighting started for real around the tenth century in the "European neighbourhood." And it went on and on.

Cr: What went on and on?

Qc: The rivalry and fighting. At family gatherings, we have always heard unflattering stories and jokes about the English people. This built serious rivalry with the English. As children, we believed what our parents told us about them to be true, like any child would.

Cr: So, you thought they really meant it, didn't you?

Qc: Yes, we French kids were sure that they were undesirable people. I don't recall Mother rebuking us for making jokes openly about the English. Therefore, it was natural to hate them. Since we fought against them for so long, we saw them as our deadly enemies and we knew we could never trust them.

Cr: Did you feel the same way about other neighbours?

Qc: No! For a time England occupied 50 percent of our land, until Jeanne d'Arc claimed she had a vision from God to raise an army and deliver us from England. This proved we could neither trust the English nor turn our back on them, Mother said. With other neighbours, as long as they did not come too close, there was no real problem.

Cr: Was that occupation long ago?

Qc: Yes, that was in our early childhood.

Cr: Can you tell me how you came to know America?

Qc: Mother needed to expand the family business and secure our future, as I said. The family was really growing, and our parents wanted new sources of food and supplies. This is what got our family involved in the race for the New World.

Cr: The race for the New World?

Qc: Our Roman Catholic neighbours, Spain and Portugal, were engaged in discovering the New World. They had special permission from the pope. Mother did not like it. No other country was allowed to get into the race. That monopoly given by the pope was not fair!

Cr: How did your parents react to this? Weren't they Roman Catholic too?

Qc: Yes, they were part of the same Roman Catholic religion, but the pope was threatening excommunication of whoever would disobey or oppose. You need to know that he had his hand on the whole world at the time.

Cr: Did your parents disobey?

Qc: Mother had her mind made up. She invented a convincing scheme and then met with the pope. This plan was to travel the seas, find new routes to new lands and bring Catholicism to the New World.

Cr: What about the other Roman Catholic children?

Qc: We were happy that the English were left out of the race by the pope. Mother hoped that her creative proposal would turn into our profit while others were eliminated from the race for good. We found out it was not the case, though.

Cr: What happened?

Qc: The English rebelled against Rome, challenging and then denying the pope's authority.

Cr: Were they excommunicated?

Qc: What we knew is they abandoned the Roman Catholic family and started their own religion. They were also called "Protestants" because of their rebellious "protest" against the pope.

Cr: How did the pope come to accept your Mom's plan?

Qc: In fact, the new pope, Clement VII, gave a fresh interpretation of the earlier 1493 papal decree. It opened the door for Mother France to send explorers to the New World. Once we discovered America, she worked on a plan to secure our future there. That was a neat idea.

Cr: How did the neighbours respond to your claim to have discovered America?

Qc: You know what? The old mentality of "who is going to be the best in Europe" came back again. Each one claimed the discovery of the American land mass. But Mother assured us that Jacques Cartier was the first in 1534. To make sure all other neighbours would notice, he planted a cross at Gaspé, on which was written, "Long live the king of France!"

Cr: If I understand well, your relatives tried to find routes to the Far East, but they found America instead.

Qc: Correct.

Cr: What was their reaction when they discovered America?

Qc: It did not take too much exploration before they realized the potential of the fur trade. Mother said she wanted to leave us a good inheritance. "We would like you to go to America, since there are real possibilities there for business and prosperity for your future." She also had the blessing of Clement VII to send more explorers and settlers. America was our future destination. It was thrilling.

Cr: All right. Moving on, how would you characterize your childhood? Were you happy?

Qc: *Yes*! I was a happy child. We felt Mom was a caring and protecting parent. It was interesting to see how we grew as a family. Mom said that our family's consistent growth made our neighbours nervous. We could play sometimes with Roman Catholic kids, but the game was always a form of "who is going to win" over the others. A spirit of competition led us to fight regularly with each other. But as a whole, I have good memories and stories from my childhood. It was fun playing. And, you know what? We felt we were winners as children and as a family!

[*Pause...*]

But...something I got from reading, something I recall really shocked me....

Cr: Do you want to talk about it?

Qc: It's about Jeanne d'Arc.

Cr: You are talking about the famous Joan of Arc who led the French army.

Qc: Yes. She was an amazing personality. After she had delivered our family (France) from the enemy (England), our mother never protected her when she was accused of witchcraft, which was only an excuse, a political plot, to give her the death penalty as they would for someone found guilty of treachery. And you know what, the one who was given the mission of procuring her and setting up a trial was French bishop Pierre Cauchon.

Cr: That sounds like an ecclesiastical court case.

Qc: How could this be?

Cr: How did the children react to this?

Qc: We were confused about this sudden, hostile accusation as if she had been an enemy. It still does not make sense! I can see the scenario even now....

Cr: Tell me about it.

Qc: I remember when the whole French family acclaimed that great woman Jeanne d'Arc after she led the French army to victories over England. She was then our "saviour"! Ironically, I also recall the scene where she was burning in a public place after being sentenced to death for heresy.

Cr: These memories are hard for you.

Qc: At the time I could not understand how we French people could be helpless spectators watching the murder of a family member, especially Jeanne d'Arc; after all, she was our dear sister and a gifted woman who did so much for us, although it was unusual to see a woman commanding and leading the army. The silence of civil and religious French authorities spoke out loud: it was like accepting the murder of one of our own French generals. How could Pierre Cauchon, a Roman Catholic bishop, play such a key role in this? We heard he loved politics and was a long-time supporter of English people. How could this be? I must be missing part of the story that would help me to make sense out of this. I am still totally confused.

[*Pause...*]

Cr: Did you talk to your Mother about it?

Qc: Never. We could not question our parents when they made a decision. Also, we could see Mother and the Church were two partners closing their eyes on this tragedy. After Jeanne d'Arc was burnt, they both warned the family, "See, any French child involved in witchcraft in the future will get the same treatment!" So, one did not feel like questioning the clergy in any way, and we did not see too many French women risk taking a role in leadership, either.

Cr: What kind of occult activities was Jeanne d'Arc involved in?

Qc: We did not know Jeanne d'Arc was involved in such activities. [*Pause.*] We have never been told. All we knew is that she said she had a vision from God to take command of the army to deliver France from our enemy. She had so much courage; she was a powerful model for our soldiers. And she really succeeded. Why did they kill her? [*Pause.*]

Cr: How did you feel about not being able to talk about this with your parents?

Qc: What are you suggesting? Should I be mad at them?

Cr: I am simply trying to help you explore how these events influenced your relationships with your parents.

Qc: Does it really matter? [*Quebec is seemingly denying that something is wrong with his relationship with his Mother.*] After all, I just mentioned I had a good childhood in Europe. It was great family time. In every family there are always little misunderstandings. We are no different than other families...It's okay! Mother was okay! Nobody is perfect anyway. She did all she could to manage the family well and to secure our future, and this is all that really counts! I have turned the page on all this....

Cr: Hmm!

Qc: You know what? If we get into the details and stories of my life, it will take as much time to share as the time we took to navigate the Atlantic Ocean! We will be meeting forever...

[*The counsellor can see Québec is not at ease here, but takes note of this and moves on to another subject.*]

## SAILING THE ATLANTIC OCEAN TO AMERICA

Cr: Speaking of your boat trip across the Atlantic, what was it like?

Qc: It seemed like eternity...an experience I am not willing to repeat.

Cr: I doubt you could repeat eternity even if you wanted to! [*They laugh.*]

Qc: It was not only long. Food and water were rationed. We were afraid of illness, too. Anyway, when someone got sick he had to be quarantined. And the waves…If you get seasick, don't ever make this trip. Horrible!

Cr: How did people get along with each other on this long trip?

Qc: "*Comme si, comme ça!*"

Cr: It was not exactly family time?

Qc: We had to deal with one more surprise. On the boat we discovered Huguenots.

Cr: Huguenots?

Qc: They were French people rebelling against our Roman Catholic religion!

Cr: You mean they did not follow the Roman Catholic way?

Qc: *Worse*, they rejected and denied our dear Roman Catholic faith and changed to another religion. With the continuing blessing of Cardinal Richelieu, Mother, the proud *fille ainée de Rome* (eldest child of Rome) did everything possible to exterminate Protestants from the family.

Cr: Was something wrong with them that they would be persecuted and marked for extermination?

Qc: Remember what was done to Jeanne d'Arc because she was involved in religious activities not approved by the Roman Catholic clergy?

Cr: Yes. Are you suggesting that Protestantism is a false religion?

Qc: Oh yes, no doubt about that. The pope and our parents were certain that these Protestants were condemned to hell, and this was preached from the pulpit.

Cr: So you started to believe this yourself?

Qc: You know what? In many families there are "rebellious children." The Huguenots were that to our family, and they divided us. Instead of obeying at home, they listened to other neighbours, who also were influenced by the evil wind of rebellion called the Protestant Reformation. They had the support of these enemy neighbours, especially the English, who had joined the Protestants themselves. Time has proven again and again that rebellious people denying the pope's authority only cause problems and divisions in our Great Roman Catholic family.

Cr: So how did this affect your French family?

Qc: Well, I just told you!

Cr: Tell me more. [*They laugh.*]

Qc: Mother was determined to eliminate them in order to stop this contamination. "If they are not stopped, we cannot be one strong family [nation]." This was the mindset of Cardinal Richelieu, who worked hard for the family's unity. We had enough challenge to hold back the English. We did not need rebellious people right among us. Cardinal Richelieu was protecting our family from other evil European influences, like that heretic Luther, whose infection spread to others, including our own Jean Calvin. And see the results: after he got contaminated, his rebellion was unstoppable.

Cr: Why were Huguenots on the boat?

Qc: The first boats that crossed the ocean were filled with people looking for adventure, prisoners, "*les filles du Roi*,"[45] Huguenots—they were the "guinea pigs" for France's venture in the New World. They all had something in common; they were looking for a new freedom.

Cr: And you too?

Qc: Well, sort of. We went there to do business ...In the midst of this motley mismatch of people, we were told the Huguenots were skilled navigators chosen to conduct us safely to America; we could handle this. But they also brought their marine crew with them. We could understand the need for proven navigators given the risk involved, but to carry other Protestants among us did not make sense at all.

Cr: How did you find out there were Huguenots on board?

Qc: During the expedition, at times French Catholics were dismayed and complained about people gathering to sing hymns and psalms from the Bible while sailing. It could not be us, because we were strongly forbidden to read and talk about the Bible; it must have been Huguenots. We were told that only our Roman Catholic priests could interpret the Bible. But can you imagine the scenario: two religious opponents sharing a ship in the middle of the ocean?

Cr: Did your mother tell you about their presence on board before the expedition left France?

Qc: Not a word. If she knew, which I'm not sure about, she might have accepted what we now call a "reasonable accommodation." Mom never talked about it before the expedition, anyway. Likely she would have been uncomfortable entering into such an arrangement, had she actually known. In any event, we had our Roman Catholic priests on board to protect against false teachings and evil people. Before we left, I recall Mother saying as we got on the boat, "We are proud of you, children!" The one thing that really mattered to her was to get us to America to expand the great family business in New France.

Cr: And you arrived in America?

Qc: *Oui*, finally...

Cr: Good! Let's us stop here for today. We will take it from here next session.

Qc: All right!

Cr: To prepare for the next session I want you to concentrate on another season of your life: adolescence (in North America, 1600–1760). We had a good session.

Qc: Thanks for the encouragement. I do not see yet where we are going, but I trust you in the process. Anyway, I enjoyed this meeting today. It is good to talk openly to someone once in a while.

[44] This attribute was ascribed to France for being faithful and a fortress for Roman Catholicism.

[45] This translates to "daughters of the king," marriageable females not needed in France.

# CHAPTER 4

# HISTORICAL INSIGHTS

## NEW FRANCE—THE COLONY THAT BIRTHED QUEBEC AND CANADA 1600–1760

⚜

IN THE VERY LATE 1500S, A HUGUENOT ENTREPRENEUR, PIERRE DU Gua de Mons (Sieur de Mons), was given a ten year monopoly by King Henri VII in the French fur business. De Mons' fur and general trading society was extensive, with a number of French ports and the shipping necessary to service them, and included several Huguenot partners. His first trip to the New World took him to Acadia (present-day Nova Scotia) in 1599. In 1603, he was made Lieutenant General of New France.

PIERRE DUGUA SIEUR DE MONS WAS GENERAL LIEUTENANT OF NEW FRANCE 1603–1612 – HE STAYED IN TADOUSSAC IN 1600

In that capacity, de Mons commissioned a well known seafaring explorer, Samuel de Champlain, to establish Quebec (city), the first permanent settlement in Canada. Champlain had started life as a Huguenot soldier in the Wars of the League. These religious wars were an attempt to suppress Protestant faith in France, as it was considered dangerous to the country's stability. In 1598, after converting to Roman Catholicism,[46] Champlain became a mariner and sailed for several years.[47] His experience and skills led him to work as an explorer serving France. He welcomed Protestants on his ship when he sailed for the New World. Du Gua de Mons sent him to New France on a mission to build a *habitation*—a station to stimulate colonization and business. Quebec City's date of birth was July 3rd, 1608. Through that accomplishment, de Champlain was called the father of New France by early Roman Catholic writers.

The king had given de Mons the mission of implementing the Roman Catholic religion among the Indians; surprisingly, he was also given permission to practice Calvinist (Huguenot) faith there.[48] While his colony was on the path to success, the revocation of his monopoly in 1607 stopped his business enterprise.[49] Cardinal Richelieu created the *Cent Associés* Company to replace and eliminate Huguenots from New France's business and colonization.[50] This terminated the work of Du Gua de Mons and was a great setback to the first significant effort to colonize New France. The plan to eliminate Huguenots was affirmed in 1627, when, as already noted, Cardinal Richelieu had the inhabitants of La Rochelle murdered en masse; La Rochelle was the strategic Huguenot fortress, business centre and training site in France. Richelieu considered La Rochelle to be a sort of nation within the Nation of France.

The first French Canadian writers (historians) needed to be Roman Catholic and French to qualify for appointment; they were hired to promote the cause of the Mother country and the Church. Historian Robert Larin mentions new impartial studies—well documented through archives—of credible historians that are now concluding that Du Gua de Mons had been unjustly forgotten and should be considered the founder and father of New France.[51] Had his Protestant faith something to do with all this? Religious intolerance left its marks everywhere.

FIRST TRADING POST BUILT IN 1600 BY PIERRE CHAUVIN
PHOTO TAKEN AT TADOUSSAC, QC, TOURIST TRADING POST

MAP DESIGNED BY CHAMPLAIN WHEN HE CAME TO TADOUSSAC IN 1603

French settlers periodically arrived and settled in present-day Nova Scotia, which the Mother country called *Acadia*. These settlements were fragile at first, and some failed, but ultimately a colony took hold in which trading with Indians—European goods for furs—and farming were the economic bases. It is estimated that before 1700 around 17,000 people went to New France,[52] but two-thirds stayed a few years only, struggling to stay alive in that hostile land. The cold winters were far harsher than those in France. Until the 1759 Conquest by Britain, most governmental effort went to serve the fur trade, often at the expense of French colonists.

Although the Mother country was glad for the treasures the land produced, she did not give much nor consistent support to her young child. It never got a genuine army; nor did it receive adequate economic help. France purposely kept it totally dependent upon her so as to profit from the colony's resources and enrich metropolitan France—a pattern common to most colonizers. Her kings were too busy solving their problems in Europe to have much inclination to spend time and funds helping a foreign colony. Their main interest was in the fur trade, abundant catches of fish and other resource wealth that they could get from that land. When they did send out governors to oversee the settlements, many of these men were inadequate but opportunist leaders, like Intendant Bigot for instance, who apparently built a corrupt fortune by manipulating the colony's finances. The colonists had to stay alive by any means they could, often with the help and counsel of compassionate Native people who knew the land and how to wrest a living from it. After the death in 1628 of Louis Hébert, the first skilled French agriculturalist with a vision for colonization,

> successive companies which ruled the destiny of New France at this time period made no effort to carry out the promise of colonization which they had given in exchange for a monopoly of fur trade, since they would thus defeat the main purpose.[53]

Because of France's negligent attitude toward her colony, her settlements continued to be fragile, and some even died out for lack of colonists. By 1643, New France had only 300 settlers.[54] For most French people, leaving the home country was costly. Only prisoners, undesirable French people, adventurers, women who agreed to marry colonial men and Huguenots looking to get away from persecution in France could find some advantage by crossing the Atlantic Ocean; apart from them, the prospect of moving to America needed some special motivation—a sort of mission mindset. It was a hard and sacrificial lifestyle, barely enabling colonists to survive. Also, because of the effect on the French economy caused by the emigration of Huguenots, France held back from encouraging more emigration because she would risk further weakening her economy and position in European business. Thereafter, the careless attitude of the Mother country allowed New France to be vulnerable to falling into the hands of the British Empire.

## THE CHURCH'S INVOLVEMENT

In this vacuum of political leadership, the Roman Catholic Church took over the administration of the colony. As pointed out earlier, never had it been the main concern of the Mother country to bring the Catholic religion to the aboriginals. Christianization[55] was envisioned in the latter seventeen century, when colonial policy was to extend exclusively Roman Catholic faith to everyone, including Natives.

Roman Catholic missionaries were well known for their relational skills and language acquisition. Several priests, probably adventurous in nature and gifted in languages, played a role in developing the fur commerce by accompanying the *coureurs des bois* (trappers) in their attempts to discover new fur territory. The

> French were first of all explorers and exploiters of the natural resources of the New World; and the great missionary effort of the seventeenth century was not unrelated to the necessity of winning the support of Indians, whose goodwill was vital to the fur trade.[56]

In New France history, Ville-Marie (today Montreal) became the first truly Catholic religious mission established in the colony of New France, as late as 1642.[57]

THE CROSS ON MONT-ROYAL IN REMEMBRANCE OF PAUL CHOMEDEY, SIEUR
DE MAISONNEUVE, WHO PLANTED A CROSS THERE IN 1643

One Roman Catholic religious order that accepted the challenge of developing France's colony in America was the Jesuits, "The Society of Jesus." After the temporary, first conquest of New France by the British (1629-32), the Jesuits' powerful influence laid a strong foundation for the Church, and their zealous efforts resulted in a religious monopoly through New France.[58]

In 1674, Monseigneur François de Laval became the first bishop of New France. His vision was to establish a powerful Roman Catholic Church under the leadership of the Jesuits. Known for his controlling and powerful personality, Laval opposed those who traded brandy to the Indians, threatening excommunication and demanding civil penalties for some of the wealthiest and most respected citizens. But "liquor had become an essential article in the fur trade; if the French had no brandy to offer, the English got the best furs with their rum."[59] The fur trade was a different reality: settlers were in America for business. Laval quarrelled with four governors, pursued the work of driving out the Huguenots and opposed other Roman Catholic missionary orders.

70

While their relations served to arouse the Mother country's interest in the colony and to bring a stream of missionaries and donations out of France, the Jesuits barred the Huguenots, who had thus far played considerable part in New France, and soon crowded out their clerical rival, the Recollets..."[60]

Bishop Laval had some friends in high places,[61] and he and the Jesuits gave New France its strong Roman Catholic foundation. New France's governor, Louis de Buade de Frontenac, ironically admitted that the church was "a machine that was leading all the rest of the colony" while he rebuked the Jesuits for "showing more zeal in capturing beavers than the souls of the Indians."[62]

A positive Jesuit priority and accomplishment was to set up a system of education and establish hospitals. They persuaded Marie de l'Incarnation to come with other Ursuline nuns to start a mission school for Indian girls. They also brought *les hospitalières* to take charge of Quebec's medical work. Jeanne Mance established a hospital in Montreal—the only apostolic one in all New France.[63] She was known for her courage and strength; she won the confidence of the Indians with her love-in-action spirit. Another nun, Marguerite Bourgeois, also established a strong mission among the settlers. Schools, hospitals and social work were all under the care and control of the Church. Mason Wade recorded, "By 1663 there were some 150 members of Catholic religious communities out of a population of about 1,500 in Quebec."[64] A strategic initiative by the Church in the colony was the establishing of parishes—"social cells"—a key contribution to the vitality of the colony, observed historian Lionel Groulx.[65] On the counsel of the priests, French Canadians began to live in rural areas, where they became known as *paysans* (peasants) or *habitants*. The clergy knew that it was important to bind the French to the land and instill into their minds the values of agriculture, self-sufficiency and supportive neighbourly love.[66] This policy was vital to birthing the Roman Catholic parishes and their growth into strong communities; they became the strategic places that would assure the survival of a French nation.

71

From the 1640s onwards, the church building and the weekly meeting became the centre of the colonists' world. They attended mass regularly, and afterwards they would gather on the porch to socialize with each other. There they learned to think alike, act alike, believe alike. Parishioners became a closely knit group. Their conviction seemed to be this: "From the beginning of New France in America, we have been learning to live as one community, to speak one language, to adopt one belief, practice one religion and live one set of moral standards. Living in the parish, we are united in one spirit." One way of thinking was helpful in resolving any problem that may arise.

It was from Roman Catholic clergy that the French gained this mindset through the weekly preaching of the priests at church. Of course, with no radio, TV or Internet, no other message could compete with the weekly pulpit sermon and influence French Canadians' minds. Thus the people became religiously united according to the well-known slogan: "One language, one religion, one country." This motto became a driving force towards the colony's survival and its dream to become a French nation.

Historian Marcel Trudel noted the distinction and the dynamism of the Roman Catholic Church in establishing within the colony many social and spiritual services and a well-built religious organization. He found it regrettable that the colonizing and the economic development did not experience the same vigorous efforts. Of course, France was more preoccupied by the fur business, he concluded.[67]

The absolutism and autocracy of the Mother country affected every aspect of the life of the colony, but the needs of New France were often neglected by a monarch more concerned with Europe than America.[68]

The consistently uncooperative attitude of the king of France was reflected amongst the people around him.

Canada was commonly regarded in worldly France as the last resort of the ruined, the alternative to a prison cell, under both Louis XIII and Louis XIV, long before Voltaire dismissed it as "several acres of snow."[69]

In the way its relationship and communication with New France were managed, France succeeded at giving the wrong impression "as if colonization and the fur business were naturally incompatible."[70] Nevertheless the fur kept coming consistently to enrich metropolitan France.

### HUGUENOTS DREAM TO COLONIZE NEW FRANCE

We've noted earlier that the Roman Catholic Church prevented Huguenots from immigrating to New France. Was France really committed to developing a viable colony in America? France seemed to be focused in another direction—specifically on eliminating anything that would keep the fur trade from enriching the Mother country at the lowest cost possible; this included the possible expansion of Protestant faith and even the development of self-sufficiency in the colony.

Kings Louis XIII and Louis XIV used culture and language to govern, responding to the Roman Catholic clergy's requests.[71] It was at the core of Cardinal Richelieu's strategy to keep the French nation from "Protestant error." Naturally, the French Catholics came to America with this mindset of religious intolerance. It was part of their spiritual heritage. They knew the Huguenots were dreaming of a new nation of religious freedom and economic opportunity. But in the New World they met persecution just as they had in France. This religious intolerance was the result of a strong alliance of spiritual and temporal power, an authority that would not allow the conscience and intelligence to breathe, according to R.P. Duclos.[72] During this era, Jesuit priests taught the laity that every creed that was not Roman Catholic was a cult from the devil.[73]

Living on farms in homogeneous parishes, isolated from any English or Huguenot merchants, Roman Catholics were denied the opportunity of learning business and management skills, even though Huguenot ability in trades and business enabled them to occupy key positions during the early colonization of New France.[74] Priests saw not only Protestant ideology but also secular knowledge and skills as threats to the ethos and continuity of the Roman Catholic parishes. For the clergy, the parishes were ideal social units to keep their hands on the parishioners.

Although, as noted earlier, the Jesuits did a great deal to establish and nurture settlements for France, their antagonism to colonists of other beliefs detracted from success in building a nation. In 1661 Bishop Laval informed Rome about Louis XIV's commitment to preventing Huguenots from getting established in New France. He recommended barring their presence altogether. In 1683, the bishop would receive confirmation that Huguenots would not be able to emigrate to New France.[75]

Much earlier, at the outset of New France under Huguenot Sieur de Mons, as we have already seen, France's Cardinal Richelieu had cancelled the mandate of de Mons' trading and shipping enterprise by creating *Les Cents Associés* (Company of 100 Associates). Only Roman Catholic businessmen could invest and have partnership in *Les Cents Associés*. Eventually it failed. Some bad timing, the British Conquest and occupation of New France (1629-32), several financial losses, expeditions that failed, and the lack of relevant and consistent support from France caused its failure. Its only lasting success was to shut out the Huguenots from New France's fur trade.

The control of fur and religion in New France was the main preoccupation of the Mother country. The French court and the Roman Catholic Church under Cardinal Richelieu had set this direction early on when the contrasting Huguenot dream seemed to be materializing. But this step was taken despite the reality that French Catholics did not emigrate easily. In contrast, the French Huguenots had been strongly motivated to move to New France.[76]

Historian François Xavier Garneau deplored religious fanaticism, especially with "French taking arms against French and deteriorating France at the profit of her enemy."[77] He continues,

> Richelieu made a big error when he consented to the way Protestants were excluded from New France. If it had been necessary to expel one of the two religions, it would have been better, in the interests of the colony, to have the expulsion fall on Roman Catholics who hardly emigrate; he brought a fatal stroke against Canada in formally closing the door to

Huguenots through the act of establishing the Company of 100 Associates.[78]

Garneau got in trouble with the Roman Catholic clergy for such writings.

Charlevoix mentions that shortly after the Jesuits took over the control of the settlements, Huguenots had emigrated mostly to the south or been exiled or put to death.[79]

With the lost of Acadia (1713 Treaty of Utrecht) as well as the eviction of the Huguenots, France surely disqualified herself from the quest of controlling all Europe and of maintaining her colony in America. "How could such fanaticism be forgiven," continues Garneau, "when it so painfully and sadly set the destiny of a whole nation, to the extent of threatening its very future?"[80] Roman Catholic writer Chanoine Lionel Groulx writes that the founding of a French Canada might have been accomplished by the spread of the French population across the country, and that the Huguenots could have played a major role in the development of the nation.[81]

The reality was that

> religious intolerance pronounced the downfall of the French colonial system in North America. The exclusion of the Huguenots from New France was one of the most stupendous blunders that history records...Industrious and thrifty, and anxious in spite of any sacrifice to enjoy the liberty of conscience denied them at home, they would have rejoiced to build up a French state in the New World.[82]

"By closing Canada to the flow of Huguenot refugees...the French destroyed their only hope for mass emigration to the New World."[83] It also opened the door for Huguenots to emigrate to England and her American colonies. From 1632 to 1760, the Canadians had increased to a total population of only 65,000, while the English colonies in America had grown to number 1,250,000. Was the population of New France therefore destined to remain both small and underdeveloped?

New research is leading historians to write on how Huguenot values and lifestyle impacted communities positively everywhere they emi-grated.[84] With their exile, both France and New France were greatly weakened.

## MOTHER COUNTRY'S NEGLECT PAVED THE WAY FOR ENGLISH CONQUEST

After the 1629-32 English occupation, New France was demon-strably vulnerable; regrettably, France failed to learn from England's brief conquest—too little was done to strengthen the colony itself, despite France and England's military and commercial competition.

During the seventeenth and eighteenth centuries, their rivalry to gain North America erupted in four major wars: King William's War of 1689-1697; Queen Anne's War of 1702-1713 (also called the War of the Spanish Succession); King George's War of 1744-1748; and the Seven Years War of 1754-1763 (includes the French and Indian War). The out-comes of each created a see-saw redistribution of North America, until finally the British wrestled from France control of the settled portion and the potential for much more of the northern land mass of the New World.

While France was attempting to establish colonies for fur trade in the New World, England was also planting settlements, both in Newfoundland and down the Atlantic coast. Since these two countries were in competition in Europe, naturally the struggle was carried over into North America. France claimed all the land drained by the rivers her men had explored, including those in the present-day USA. The English claimed territory that overlapped that of the French. Since borders through forest and uncharted regions were vague, hostilities frequently broke out. The French raided American towns and the English Americans captured French territory.

Nothing was gained in all these skirmishes, however. In each case, all conquered lands were returned through treaties, but rivalry for the fur trade and battles for commerce with the Natives and fishing rights in the Atlantic continued, heightening the animosity in the long-standing con-flict. For decades and lifetimes, not only the colonists but also the Native people had to endure the insecurity and suffering brought on by these conflicts.

Still preoccupied by her homeland ambitions, the Mother country did not envision any significant future for Quebec, even though its economy was finally starting to show a modest beginning.

Shipyards, factories and sawmills began to operate along the St. Lawrence River. Forges at St. Maurice were producing stoves, pots, ploughshares, tools and anchors by 1738. Four years earlier, the Chemin du Roi ("King's highway") was completed—the first road between Montreal and Quebec. The production of wheat, hemp and flax had tripled between 1721 and 1739.[85]

France failed to see the potential, and the neglect continued. In fact, the Roman Catholic Church stepped in to help, since "it was the Church, rather than the monarchy or the trading companies, which gave the colony the support it needed during this difficult early period."[86]

France was indifferent towards her colony since she signed the 1713 Treaty of Utrecht, giving away Hudson Bay, Newfoundland and most of Acadia, which allowed England to take full control of the seas. This treaty crippled New France's trade with France as well as her security. "The military question was acute. France's royal troops had dwindled to a mere 600, many of that number being old men and boys; reinforcements from France were refused."[87] Rudimentary defence had to be organized by local police in each parish, while New France had to cope with a growing English military force in the colonies to the south. The potential for gaining control of the economy in Quebec could only encourage the English toward the eventual invasion of New France and the fulfillment of their great dream to have all of North America.

Conflict in North America broke out in 1754, two years before the Seven Years War broke out in Europe, and is known as the French and Indian War. What happened in North America was indeed decisive, altering the course of world history. William Pitt, the British secretary of state, planned to cripple France by striking at her colonies, and he increased Britain's strength in North America to 23,000 soldiers. This was in contrast to New France's respectable but severely outnumbered 6,800. Quebec begged for more military aid, but France informed Governor Marquis de Vaudreuil that no warships would be sent to the colony—

which meant no more supplies. The skirmishes of the 1750s had depleted their economy and left them helpless.

British soldiers, American colonists and Indian bands friendly to the English were on the march toward New France. They defeated the French in Acadia on July 26, 1758, taking control once again—permanently this time—of the fortress of Louisbourg, France's last strategic military post on the Gulf. With this protection gone, the St. Lawrence was under British control and open to invasion. As General Wolfe sailed toward Quebec with 168 warships and 39,000 men (including 9,000 soldiers),[88] French Canadians, feeling weak everywhere, sensed the likely end of their dream, New France.

In 1759, the British strategically scaled the heights onto the Plains of Abraham above the Quebec citadel, and on the *Champs de Bataille* (battlefields), General Montcalm and his French army were defeated. In this battle Quebec was lost in a few minutes, the French Canadians were confused and their dream was shattered. In 1760, Montreal also fell to the English, and three years later, by the terms of the Treaty of Paris of 1763, the king of France yielded without restriction and handed all New France lands and his loyal subjects over to Britain, with the exception of the tiny St. Pierre and Miquelon islands in the Gulf of St. Lawrence. These assured France of fishing rights and a convenient operational base in North America. England got far more than France, but the real loss was reserved for *les Québécois*, whose dream had been to have complete control of their affairs and to be a nation in America.

French Canada feared it would lose everything. It was frightening. From their past experience of war, they knew that when a nation is conquered it submits and becomes assimilated into the culture of its conquerors. They also saw what the French and English had done to the Natives in America—how they took their land and possessions, exploiting and assimilating them, ravaging their culture and identity. "French Canadian apprehensions were not felt in vain," wrote Chanoine Groulx. "They knew instinctively that freedom of conscience was hardly possible in Catholic and Protestant countries."[89] They also remembered that under the command of the king and Cardinal Richelieu, they had attempted to eliminate the Huguenots—French people of their own blood. Now, being imprisoned in the cell of the conquered automatically raised haunting memories and fear of those tragic experiences. Would there be retaliation in kind? No wonder the French Canadians trembled. They felt that the worst would come to them soon.

Indeed, tremendous changes lay ahead, not only for Quebec but for all North America, changes that would shape the future of the world itself.

✂ ————————————————————

46    Champlain gave the name of Ste. Hélène to an island close to Montreal to honour his wife, Hélène.

47    Wade, *French Canadians*, p. 9. Larin and Trudel are also convinced Champlain was a Huguenot who converted to Roman Catholicism (Larin, *Brève Histoire*, p. 68). In fact, he married Hélène de Champlain, who was Roman Catholic (Ibid..)

48    Larin, *Brève Histoire*, p. 64.

49    Trudel, *Initiation*, p. 51.

50    Larin, *Brève Histoire*, p. 18.

51    Larin, *Brève Histoire*, p. 16. Larin mentions historians Marcel Trudel, Jean Glenisson and H.P. Biggar. Larin listed credible historians whose studies support this thesis: Marcel Trudel, Jean Glenisson, Robert Leblanc, Samuel Elliot Mori, George MacBeathson.

52    Lalonde, *Des loups dans la bergerie*, p. 31.

53    Ibid., p. 15.

54    Wade, *French Canadians*, pp. 13-14,

55    During that era, it meant recruiting people to join the Catholic religion.

56    Wade, *French Canadians*, p. 4.

57    Trudel, *Initiation*, p. 57.

58    Wade, *French Canadians*, p. 14.

59    Ibid., p. 21.

60    Ibid., p. 15.

61    Canadian Automobile Association and The Reader's Digest Association, *Heritage of Canada*, p. 60.

62    Duclos, *Histoire du protestantisme*, p. 44.

63    Trudel, *Initiation*, p. 57.

64    Wade, *French Canadians*, p. 16.

65    Lionel Groulx, *Histoire du Canada français depuis la découverte* (Tome II), p. 35.

66    Duclos, *Histoire du protestantisme*, p. 19.

67    Trudel, *Initiation*, p. 61.

68    Wade, *French Canadians*, p. 3.

69    Ibid.

70    Ibid., 9.

71    Larin, *Histoire Brève*, p. 42.

72    Duclos, *Histoire du protestantisme*, p. 25.

73    This teaching continued until Vatican II; in the 1990s, Pope Jean Paul II called all professing Catholics to now welcome Protestants and Bible-believing Christians into "Christianity."

74    Lalonde, *Des loups dans la bergerie*, p. 30.

75    Larin, *Brève Histoire*, p. 101.

76    Duclos, *Histoire du protestantisme*, p.32. Quoting Parkman, *The Old Regime—Frontenac*, p. 416.

77    Gaudette, *Guerres de Religion*, p. 44. Quoting François-Xavier Garneau, *Histoire du Canada* [History of Canada], (Paris: Alcan, 1928), vol. 1, p. 108.

78    François-Xavier Garneau, *Histoire du Canada depuis sa découverte jusqu'à nos jours* [History of Canada from its discovery to the present day], (Quebec: Imprimerie de N Aubin, 1845-46), vol. 1, p. 156.

79    Duclos, *Histoire du protestantisme*, p. 22.

80    Garneau, *Histoire du Canada*, Vol. 1, p. 317.

81    Groulx, *Histoire du Canada français*, p. 11.

82    Baird, Charles W., *History of the Huguenot Emigration to America* (Baltimore: Regional Publishing Company, 1966), vol. I, p. 116.

83    Leslie Choquette, *Frenchmen into Peasants* (Cambridge and London: Harvard University Press, 1997), p. 282.

84    For more information, please visit the National Huguenot Society's web site at http://www.huguenot.netnation.com.

85    CAA and RDA, *Heritage of Canada*, p. 105.

86    Wade, *French Canadians*, p. 14.

87    Ibid., 30.

88    Trudel, *Initiation*, p. 104.

89    Groulx, *Histoire du Canada français*, p. 28.

# CHAPTER 5

# "JE ME SOUVIENS..."

## FRENCH CANADIANS' ATTEMPT TO TAME AMERICA
## 1600–1760

❧

*[Counselling in progress...]*

Cr: How are you today?

Qc: Not too good. To be honest, I did not feel like coming here today.

Cr: Has anything special happened?

Qc: It's okay. I am here. Let's just get started....

Cr: [*The counsellor opens the discussion, knowing from experience that whatever concerns Quebec will surface sooner or later.*] Any subject you want to start with? It might be something from your homework.

Qc: Let's just take it from where we were last session.

Cr: Okay. You talked about a long and challenging trip across the Atlantic Ocean and how happy you were when you set foot in America.

Qc: *Oui!* Finally....

Cr: A new season of life was starting, I guess.

Qc: It was challenging to get into this new life, and now I realize how risky it was. Anyway, we had to make up our mind to step on board that ship. It didn't look like it would get us there. Crossing the Atlantic was no honeymoon!

[*The counsellor gestures with empathy.*] We got to New France without dying anyway. We desperately wanted a fresh start. Even though we felt somehow trapped and away from civilized life, we really did not want to go back in Europe. We had no time for self-pity; we had to fight against the hungry insect life and diseases and to prepare for the cold winter coming. We'd heard about the unbearable cold. We had to deal with Indians too....

## DEALING WITH INDIANS

Cr: How was the contact with the Indians?

Qc: It started well. Overall, by what we saw and the little we had heard of these people, it seemed that they would be easy to tame.[90]

Cr: Tame? Well, perhaps that's what was needed! So you felt comfortable with them?

Qc: This was a brand new challenge for us; we did not know much, and it kept us on our toes. But we were prepared and not alone. First of all we had help from the Church; in fact, the great missionary effort of the seventeenth century was partly about winning the Indians over to us; their goodwill was vital to our fur trade.[91] Some of our colony had previously learned to approach the Indians. Mother asked them to teach us about this when we arrived in America.

Cr: In other words, you had good preparation.

Qc: Oh yes! She showed us how to tame and control the Indians.

Cr: How did this work?

Qc: We brought some gifts, which included barrels of alcohol.

Cr: Alcohol! Was it needed to fight those famous cold winters?

Qc: It was not what you think! No, it was to loosen up the Indians. It really did soften their behaviour. And those who were more resistant, well, they stayed quiet and co-operative at the sight of our guns; we got to control them as well.

Cr: How did the Indians react to this?

Qc: Positively. The reality is that, finding no treasure among the poverty-stricken northern Indians, whose struggle for basic existence made European tools and trinkets very valuable, we (the French) fell easily into the role of gods, which Indians assigned to the white newcomers.[92] But above all, alcohol really worked. They loved the feeling; after getting used to it, they just wanted more...we felt we were ready to start trading for furs.

Cr: Do you think this foundation was solid enough for you to build relationships with Indians?

Qc: We were told by Mother the stuff we brought would improve their lifestyle, also that they were not "civilized." So they needed our stuff as much as we needed their furs. Yes, on that basis we built partnership. They would go and hunt furs, for they knew how to do this, and come back and exchange their stock of furs for alcohol, trinkets and stuff. Every time they came back from hunting, it was like "party time," with eating and drinking.

Cr: Party time? What do you mean?

Qc: Let me give you an idea of what the "Fur Fair" was like. Brandy, tobacco, muskets and food attracted the Indians to trading, like flies to honey. This is how the trade ritual went:

Company officers and the Indian Chief (held) a ceremony to open trading and for several days the fort sold only brandy; two weeks of avarice and revelry were about to begin...At night they roamed the town waving tomahawks and guns, tearing off their clothes, singing, whooping, and fighting. Heads were (bashed) in, noses bitten off. That fuelled boisterous nights...Traders had stalls displaying knives, axes, muskets, and color(ful) clothing. After several days the brandy was cut off and the revels ended. Indians and company officers met again, Indians bearing a gift of beaver pelts. Then sitting in circle, whites and Indians again smoked the calumet; it was time to (begin) bartering furs...Finally the Indians left, taking their new possessions—and sometimes measles, smallpox and cholera.[93]

It was time to go back hunting again. They came back over and over. They seemed to enjoy their new lifestyle.

Cr: So, as a whole, your experience with Indians was positive.

Qc: *Oui!* Kind of.

Cr: Kind of?

PHOTO TAKEN INSIDE CHAUVIN TRADING POST, TADOUSSAC

MY WIFE LORRAINE INSIDE CHAUVIN TRADING POST

## Dealing with the English

Qc: Positive with some Indians. But there was another shocking event waiting for us.

Cr: What was it?

Qc: When we arrived in America, to our great surprise we found English people too. We just couldn't escape these threatening rivals. And, you know what, we found out they had made partners of the Iroquois Indians!

Cr: Did you not tell me in another session that England was in the race for the New World despite Roman Catholic countries having a monopoly and blessing by the pope?

Qc: Yes, but Mother told us that "we French" discovered new routes to new lands that had become our property. America was our land, she said. She told us there would be hostile Indians but never mentioned we would have to deal once more with the English. This is the last thing we desired!

Cr: Did your parents think France made exclusive discoveries?

Qc: Well, that was another miscommunication, I believe…[*Quebec looks down in an attitude of resignation.*]

Cr: How did you respond to that?

Qc: We could have phoned 911 or dashed off an e-mail to Mother in France…Seriously, just to see those English again was horrible; it resurrected bad memories.

Cr: It sounds like a cold shower.

QC: Oui! Right on! Or a *nightmare*! We could see the writing on the wall of America: "English and French Worlds in new Power Struggle."[94]

Cr: I see…this was a challenging beginning in America—dealing with Indians and English.

Qc: We found out that there were several tribes of Indians in America. Already, the English had become friends with the Iroquois who liked the English "fur trade rum!" To compete, we worked hard to make friends with other tribes, like Hurons, Abenaki, Montagnais for example, who really enjoyed our brandy. Here we were still fighting with the English again, not just to control the land but now to compete for the Indians and the fur trade. *Very frustrating!*

PHOTOS TAKEN FROM LE SITE DE LA NOUVELLE FRANCE, SAINT-FÉLIX-D'OTIS, SAGUENAY LAC ST-JEAN REGION, QC

Cr: Was the Church supporting this practice of providing brandy to Indians?

Qc: Monseigneur Laval was strongly against it, but let's be practical here—wasn't it better to let the Indians drink our brandy and become our allies for fur trade than to let them take the English rum and partner with the English to get full control of the fur trade?

[*Something big seems to bother Quebec.*]

Cr: I see you have much on your mind.

Qc: I am tired! I did not sleep well...but it's okay! I want to be here.

Cr: Okay. If we look back to our last session, am I correct in saying you had, in general, positive memories about your childhood in Europe? You said it was a good family time.

Qc: Oui! I know. I want to turn the page on my past and move forward with my life! Why should I spend my time talking about parents who let me down?

Cr: They let you down?

Qc: You know—your homework! The more I remember, the more I read about life in North America and the 1760 Conquest, the more I see how...[*moment of silence*]...How she, meaning France, abandoned me..."*Je me souviens....*"

[*The counsellor notes tears in Quebec's eyes and a pained expression.*]

Cr: I want you to know that you don't need permission to express your feelings. Believe it or not, often pain is effective in revealing insights that help us to understand what is going on deep inside. By looking at our past we can make sense of the present. This is why I asked you to do some reading about your own life story.

Qc: What do you mean? It does not make sense; it just does not make me feel good to think back to what my parents did to us, their French children. I am not a masochist!

Cr: Let me explain. Imagine a surgeon saying to his patient who is in pain, "We need to take a look at a deeper level to find and treat your pain's root cause." Perhaps it gets surgically removed. Or perhaps it can be medically healed. What we're doing is like that.

Qc: But we are not in a hospital! [*Pause.*] Or are we?

Cr: I have a question for you: Tell me what led you first to meet with me.

[*Quebec is looking once more at the window.*]

Qc: Don't really know! I think I needed to talk to someone about the stress and struggles of my life and to better understand myself.

Cr: Do we agree that your stress and struggles are causing pain? [*Quebec is now looking down, then changes position as if loosening up to talk.*] A surgeon has to get at the diseased tissue that causes the pain and deal with it before the healing process can take place. We're doing that at relational and emotional levels here. Like surgery, it can hurt...and I don't have a psychological anaesthetic, unfortunately.

Qc: Why do I have to go through this?

Cr: If a patient has no pain, the surgeon might not know something is wrong in the body. But unknown disease inevitable damages or kills. Pain actually helps the surgeon, if not the patient. Psychologically, it is the same: emotional pain—suffering—leads to understanding. [*Pause.*]

I admit surgery is never a funny thing. There is a disease called leprosy though, and it is characterized by the absence of pain, because it kills the nervous system wherever it has infected the body. A patient can't feel the pain when they injure the leprous tissue, and her body keeps getting infected and disintegrating. Do you believe with me that leprous people would see the value in recovering the ability to feel pain?

Qc: I see what you mean.

Cr: You said something like this: "*Je me souviens...*" Do you remember something?

Qc: I do remember how during fur trade, as long as we would fill the French merchant ship with furs, we would get in return stuff to help us survive. But if because of battles against English and Iroquois, or of a bad hunting season, we could not fill the boats with furs, we got into trouble. The ships carried furs to France and came back with *vivres* (things to make a living). Of course, we had to buy at very high cost the cloth, tools, and other *vivres* we needed. The French merchants took full advantage of their monopoly and our isolation.

Cr: How did you manage to make a living?

Qc: I wonder how we did. We depended on this exchange to survive the tough pioneer conditions. We had minimum tools and no experience in agriculture where much of the year is sub-zero in temperature. We were helped a lot by Indians who were willing to get us started in gardening; they introduced us to the North American crops and soil they knew well and to the bounties that could be gotten from the forest and streams. We were so busy learning, recovering from mistakes and just surviving that we did not have much time to think. Boats took months to come, and the Hochelaga River [St. Lawrence] was likely to be unnavigable because of ice for almost half the year.

Cr: This was not easy living. You must have had stress through this.

Qc: Of course it was stressful...at times frustrating.

[*Quebec is looking down again as if feeling discouraged.*]

Qc: [*After a moment of silence.*] Look what I got from my reading: the Mother country's colonial policy was to put many restrictions on New France because King Louis XIV had no genuine desire for our development; he perceived us as a potential economic competitor. That wasn't fair. New France was supposed to be *our* future. Instead, Mother was exploiting us.

Cr: Any special reason the Mother country was acting this way?

Qc: Well, she kept us tied to her apron strings because she wanted us to be totally dependent on her! From what I remember while still living in Europe, she never allowed a colony to become self-sufficient and independent from her.

Cr: She practiced the same policy toward you?

Qc: *Yes*! but we were *her children*, not colonial slaves from Africa or some other outpost, yet she treated us as just another colony forced to serve her, our very own mother.

Cr: Not much encouragement, then?

Qc: Not much from France. On the other hand, thanks be to God, the Church gave us some encouragement and coached us toward agriculture to build our future. The hard labour of farming then was really a matter of *paysan* subsistence; we barely survived when weather was good—and it was almost impossible when the harvest season had bad weather, as it too often did. We struggled along...thank God for those Indians.

Cr: You weren't sure you could survive?

Qc: Exactly. The little support we got was a big joke: the colonists who were sent here were not prepared at all to do agriculture; out of 10,000 immigrants before 1666, more than 75 percent had no experience at all in agriculture.[95] In the fur trade, we did not have much choice if we wanted to survive; we learned to live in and from nature because help never seemed to be available. We began to believe we were "born for little bread." So, being encouraged by the clergy, we worked hard to make farming and helping each other in our parish communities our lifestyle; and, after years of struggle, we got somewhere with this, and maybe it is something to be proud of.

Cr: This never became easy living, I suppose.

Qc: No. The first generations had it so tough. Many died. Even in 1663, New France was close to bankruptcy; colonizing was a failure.[96] New France's economy was based on fur alone. Prior to 1760, we experienced about fifteen years of being a colony at war, endured famine, were exploited by frauds from *l'intendant* Bigot and his associates, and lost many of our numbers to disease and harsh climate. It was too late anyway!

## THE CONQUEST: A HORRIBLE MOMENT

Cr: What do you mean by *too late*?

Qc: The more I look at it now, the more I see the odds were all against us. The fur trade was uncertain, and also it was hard to get either settlers or soldiers from the Mother country. I remember some soldiers arriving on ships only when the fur trade business was in danger. We needed more protection than that. It was too much to be serving Mother France with luxurious furs, building a colony in the harsh, isolated north, and at the same time being soldiers and developing an armed force. Time and again, our requests for more soldiers and manpower were turned down; on the other hand, the British army and the English population on the American seaboard were growing by the year.

Cr: What did you do about all that?

Qc: We were still hoping that Mother would send men to reinforce us when we heard the bad news that Louisburg was taken by 20,000

British soldiers. This closed the St. Lawrence River access to French ships. The English plan succeeded. We were cut off from the world, and 39,000 English soldiers were on their way to conquer Quebec. So, not having much choice, we did something heart-breaking: we had to arm our young teen boys in a desperate attempt to resist the enemy. To make a long story short, in 1759, our general Montcalm died in battle and we lost to the English on *Les Champs de Bataille* [the Plains of Abraham battlefield] in Quebec City. This was the second time we lost against the English.

Cr: Second time, you say?

Qc: *Oui*, the first time we were conquered was much earlier—in 1629. We knew what conquest meant as we lived for three miserable years under the English conqueror, until 1632.[97] The Treaty of St-Germain-en-Laye restored New France to Louis XIII and France.

Cr: How was your relationship with your "parents" after you were given back to them?

Qc: The first conquest was a worrisome indicator of how vulnerable we were in America. And given the problematic relationship with our French parents, this insecurity remained generation after generation. We had no real security, and we knew it.

Cr: Did your mother know about it?

Qc: I read from my notes that she had received warnings about the situation even before Pierre Le Moyne d'Iberville gave King Louis XIV his 1699 wake-up call:

If France does [not] get this part of America [Louisiana], the English colony that is growing steadily will multiply to the point that before one hundred years it will be strong enough to conquer all America. And two years later, D'Iberville went back to France with yet another prophetic warning: "The English of this continent, joined with Indians, will have the potential power on sea and land to control all America."[98]

Looking back, the Indians have actually been our most faithful partners when we needed them; they were great loyal people. D'Iberville had a heart for New France and defended our cause despite France's indifference toward it.

Cr: We can now see that D'Iberville was reading the future correctly, can't we?

Qc: What France refused to believe was possible became the reality. I see now that their long-term neglect impoverished us.[99] Colonization, beyond the little necessary to serve the fur trade, was not encouraged by the self-serving monopolists in this business. Meanwhile, New France was ruled by transient French officials looking out only for the benefit of France;[100] they were little more than opportunists.

Cr: [*Empathetically.*] It seems you were very disadvantaged.

Qc: We were, from the beginning right through to the 1759 conquest, 130 anxious years after we first fell to the English. Even today "*Je me souviens*" is a cry from the heart, reflecting the despair of a people who were set up for failure and loss.

Cr: Then what was the atmosphere after the 1759 conquest? How did the French children feel?

Qc: The second and permanent loss to Britain was the end of our world. It seemed we had lost our land, our religion, our language, our laws, and especially the pride we had felt in building something from nothing all by ourselves. In the end, we were only...losers!

Cr: Was anything different after the second invasion and defeat?

Qc: After the first defeat in 1629, we heard rumours that Mother was negotiating to have us back under her control. But after the second conquest, the next thing we heard was that a deal had been made in Europe. By it we were permanently abandoned into the hands of the English enemy. Even though we were told "Welcome" by the British government and our clergy speculated to us that the conqueror's permission would be given to speak French and stay Roman Catholic, we didn't know how and couldn't believe that this could work. It did not make sense for a conqueror at that time to give any privilege to the conquered people. We knew what we had done to the Huguenots, we knew what had been done to Native people; as a result, we believed the worst would come to us.

Cr: What do you feel concerning the Mother country? What comes to your mind?

Qc: [*Speaking slowly, then faster and vehemently.*] Lack of support, lack of soldiers, lack of trust, lack of consideration, lack of love, rejection, and I could go on and on. Listen to my reading notes [*flourishing the notes he wrote doing his homework*]. At the time when we needed the support of manpower and soldiers the most in America, we now know that 36,000 men and soldiers were busy building *Le Chateau de Versailles* [the Versailles Castle] just to please King Louis XIV. Can you believe this? Mother country refused to send any soldiers to help us save New France; the big money and manpower were diverted to indulging herself extravagantly at Versailles, abandoning France's dream for America.[101]

> The absolutism and autocracy of the Mother country affected every aspect of the life of the colony, but the needs of New France were neglected by a monarch more concerned with Europe than America.[102]

This negative attitude of King Louis XIV was discouraging his loyal subjects who sacrificially worked to enrich France's fortune. [*Shaking his head, Quebec seems devastated, emotionally drained.*]

Do you know what, Counsellor? We could not believe the things we were hearing from the other side of the ocean, even though we were padding our Mother's bank account by all the taxes levied on us. We realized then that they didn't care about us. They despised us! As the Catholic historian Chanoine Groulx mentioned, the Mother country neglected our colony because it was too expensive and not worth investing in, compared with other French colonies, like Africa.[103]

Cr: What do you conclude from this?

Qc: What we learned later is that Louis XIV faced two challenges. Here is the situation: in Europe, his empire was in eclipse; wars threatened the continent. Even more alarming, signs pointed to the coming French Revolution; the deteriorating domestic, economic, social, financial and military situation all influenced France's decisions. He wasn't prepared to deal with yet another question, which was, "is it worth supporting New France?"

Cr: A real dilemma, wasn't it?

Qc: But how come England had energy, money, supply, manpower to colonize and soldiers to invest in America while our Mother country did not? New France, suffering such military and economic insecurity,[104] needed immediate assistance; how could 65,000 peasants protect themselves against 1,500,000 English Americans in colonies that had developed a dynamic vision for their future and were equipped to make it a reality?

Cr: France's policy suffers in comparison to England's.

Qc: We heard similar complaints from the English colonies to the south against British mistreatment and exploitation; consistent frustrations opened the way for the American Revolution. But this is not what I want to talk about. I have already said that France's rulers kept us weak and dependent on her. While some French Canadians wanted to launch Jean Talon's mercantile program in order to develop New France's economy, we were forbidden to start manufacturing and developing our own businesses, for it would be seen as a threat to the economic superiority of France. In 1704, a letter from the king reminded us that a colony exists to provide *matières premières* (natural resources) to its colonial master, effectively restricting New France to remain a colony of fur.[105]

Cr: How do these historical insights make sense to you?

Qc: We were France's *victim*! Our downfall was not our fault. No wonder the French Revolution was coming! France failed not only New France; her rulers ensured that she failed herself.

Cr: So you felt you were her victim.

Qc: Look, just as a desperate mother dumps her child in a back alley for her own survival, "Mother France" chose to callously neglect and eventually abandon New France. The tragedy is that France not only rejected the child of her own blood but also discredited herself totally by selling her child for two small islands to the English, her worst long-time enemy.

Cr: It hurts to be a victim sold this way.

Qc: Now you know why I did not sleep well and considered cancelling the meeting today. As a child of such a mother I feel despised and rejected. It was abusive. You want to know how I feel? I am *angry*. I *hate* my parents...I still can't understand our Mother country abandoning her own child. Once she had called me "my dear New France." But these were just empty words, lip service. Her self-centredness went as far as *selling us*—her own children with the same French blood as she had—to the *English* government for two little plots of land just to preserve "her" fishing rights—to eat well![106] [*Pausing and breathing deeply.*] It hurts to be sold by your mother.

Cr: Remember, pain is okay; it's legitimate. Just let it out. Express your thoughts about this.

Qc: How would you like being treated like mere *merchandise*? How would *you* feel after learning from a stranger that you'd been suddenly sold to the *English* and would be living in a strange *English* foster home? Mother taught us to hate and fight the English for more than seven centuries, *oui*, 700 years...now she got rid of us as we were being handed over...discarded into English hands as a very cheap commodity. What a *nightmare*!

Cr: [*Notes more tears in Quebec's face...another long silence.*] I see what you are saying today.

Qc: You asked for my thoughts. My first thought was: Was it worth investing my life here in North America? What hope was there for us after living such a deprived lifestyle for 200 years? What a waste of life...of many lives.

Cr: You think so?

Qc: From the time we arrived in North America, my life has been a total mess; I feel lost, alone—no, worse than that: a child who's been neglected, used, abused, brutally betrayed and abandoned—then bartered away for a pittance to an enemy. I feel like an orphan.

Cr: It's like a deep, fresh wound still, isn't it?

Qc: How would you feel if it were you? How would you handle this? *I need to turn the page*!

[*Quebec silently gazes through the office window.*]

Cr: I think we could recap here. How does that sound?

Qc: I should finish. I am exhausted!

Cr: I understand. Before we close this session, please tell me what you learned.

97

Qc: "*Je me souviens....*" Mother country lied to us, schemed to benefit herself and manipulated us so that we'd serve her own selfish whims. It was a big mistake to trust my parents. My trust was broken and remains broken...She set us up to be *losers*! The only help we had was from the priests; they offered some comfort and encouragement to keep us going. I guess they had their own agenda, but I think they did care about us; they remained with us after the Conquest, helping us become survivors through the times when the high class could choose to leave America. [*Quebec pauses, consulting notes.*]

Now let me read you something that exactly expresses my heart:

When a French Canadian says, "*Je me souviens,*" he not only remembers the long, hard years of New France but also the fact that he belongs to a conquered people. It is deep in his consciousness, although he may recognize that New France was not so much conquered by the English as abandoned by France; and this is the crucial factor in his psychological makeup—and his relationship with English Canadians.[107]

PHOTO TAKEN FROM SITE DE LA NOUVELLE FRANCE, SAINT-FÉLIX-D'OTIS, SAGUENAY-LAC ST-JEAN REGION, QC

PHOTOS REPRESENT A REPLICA OF 1608 QUEBEC HABITATION

Cr: [*After a period of silence.*] I am impressed how you prepared yourself so well. Keep working at it; the journaling is good. You had amazing insights today. They should help to get some peace about what you have experienced. Probably today's session will raise a lot of questions. Don't worry; your answers will eventually fit together, like the pieces of a jigsaw puzzle. Keep up the good work! In our next session we will talk about your life after Conquest.

Qc: Thanks. It was not easy today. I hate to talk about my past and my parents. The way we were abused and exploited tears me to pieces...it breaks my heart; I will never forgive what they did...[*Shakes his head in resignation*]. I don't know, probably it's time to move on. Thanks, man...I'll see you soon.

❋ ─────────────

90    Wade, *French Canadians*, p. 7.

91    Ibid., p. 4.

92    Ibid., p. 7.

93    CAA and RDA, *Heritage of Canada*, pp. 64, 72.

94    Trudel, *Initiation*, p.76.

95    Trudel, *Initiation*, p. 219.

96    Yves Tessier, *Guide Historique de Québec*, p. 127.

97    Guy Frégault and Marcel Trudel, *Histoire du Canada par les textes*, p. 25.

98    Denis Vaugeois, *La fin des alliances franco-indiennes: Enquête sur un sauf-conduit de 1760 devenu un traité en 1990*, p. 20.

99    Trudel, *Initiation*, p. 76.

100    Wade, *French Canadians*, p. 5.

101    Dangeau, *Journal*, 1685, http://colleges.ac-rouen.fr/braque-rouen/cours/4ex/versailles/construction.htm (no longer available).

102    Wade, *French Canadians*, p. 3.

103    Groulx, *Histoire du Canada Français*, p. 24. England saw the potential and had a vision for North America.

104    Trudel, *Initiation*, p. 76.

105    Ibid., pp. 73, 213, 214.

106    The two islands are St-Pierre and Miquelon, just south of Newfoundland; they still belong to France.

107    Wade, *French Canadians*, p. 47.

# CHAPTER 6

# HISTORICAL INSIGHTS

## TOWARD SURVIVAL AFTER 1760

⚜

### TOWARD SURVIVAL

Quebec could not anticipate a positive outcome in the dark days after the Conquest. In fact, searching for any means of survival was the grim task to take up. In that era, defeat usually carried the possibility of the scattering or elimination of the conquered society and its people. The bloody Acadian tragedy was a recent case study of that very outcome.

For three years after the Conquest, the Canadian colonies were under military rule while Britain and France completed the Seven Years War and then negotiated its settlement. This finally came in 1763 through the Treaty of Paris when England was given almost everything that France had owned in North America.

That same year, the British made the Royal Proclamation, a wide-ranging document that designated the use of her newly-enlarged territories in North America. While it was in effect for only eleven years, it allocated limited land for the conquered French settlers (essentially where they had settled along the St. Lawrence River and no more), more extensive seaboard lands for the English colonies to the south, and vast, scarcely-charted inland territory for the Native tribes. Still other land in North America was claimed by Spain.

At that time, too, the name "Canada" disappeared as the tiny French colony's name; it became the Province of Quebec. Any person, English or

French, residing in the province[108] would be called "Canadian."[109] It appeared that Quebec had been stripped of much of its identity and potential. It is devastating for a nation to be in the position of loser; the natural and legitimate response is to become a self-protective survivor.

## THE 1759 PLAINS OF ABRAHAM BATTLE, A KEY SITUATION

The long background to the Conquest of Quebec left its marks. From Day One of Britain's administration of Quebec, bargaining, power struggle, competition and a demanding spirit would describe the French clergy's attitude to the British authority. The French and English were still like "cats and dogs," though now needing to live side by side in Quebec. France and Britain had been rivals for world power since the tenth century. These two opponents would now engage one another from much closer quarters! A spirit of bitterness, resentment and anger initially settled upon this newly formed Canadian blended family. One might say, "What a start!" At this point in time, one must realize how this tragic context contributed to the real foundations on which Canada would be built; it would profoundly mark the relationships among the three founding nations.

The Conquest was pivotal for North America. The future powerful and successful British Empire began with the acquisition of America. The historians have closely examined the beginning of a new relationship between the English conqueror (who would shape the continent) and the marginalized, defeated French. For some time to come, not much would be heard about the Native people. What would become of them? In fact, as the commerce of furs would slow down and the economy grow more diversified under the British regime, less attention would be given the First Nations people, who were increasingly isolated in their reserves. Relationships among French, Native and English have always been shaped by the development of businesses and the economy.

The first attempt at rapport between the French and English was some political business; it resulted in a relationship of bargaining between the two main actors—the Roman Catholic Church, who by default represented the French settlers, and the British government. The bishop was for the colony what the pope was for the entire Roman Church. So he and his clergy negotiated the right to have Roman

Catholic parishes, to speak French, to levy church taxes and other eccle-siastic privileges. In return, the bishop promised the full submission and loyalty of French Canadians to the British government.

The Roman Catholic clergy had already seen the responsibility and seized the opportunity to be become the ambassadors and negotiators for the French settlers. Who else was there to do that? They stepped up to provide leadership and gain a measure of community autonomy as they contemplated their uncertain future. "The history of Quebec since 1760 reveals how the French Canadians concentrated their resources and devoted them to the struggle of survival. This effort still continues long after survival has been assured."[110]

The English citizens in the thirteen colonies to the south expressed their disappointment with the British government, who practised, from their point of view, a policy of too-generous compromise as conqueror toward the French conquered. Why should their victorious government negotiate so generously and give such privileges to the former enemy? "The conquered should submit and somehow be assimilated!" they thought. After all, that had been the case with some Indians and the Acadians.

## ENGLAND PARENTING A BLENDED FAMILY: A REAL CHALLENGE!

Quebec was a chiefly francophone island in a large anglophone North American sea. In 1689, there were 200,000 Anglo-Americans to 10,000 French Canadians; in 1756, 1,500,000 Anglo-Americans for 70,000 French Canadians.[111] The numbers for each were larger, but the ratios almost the same, at 20 to 1 or slightly better for the English. England had never before possessed a colony of such size—65,000 people after the dust of war had settled—and of another European nationality. While the first approach was to treat the *Québécois* like a conquered people with the goal of assimilating them into English cul-ture, England was beginning to decipher a message on the wall con-cerning the American colonies; feeling used and mistreated by the British government, they would rebel just a few years later. Governor Murray saw the potential danger of losing the French Canadians through emigration as he tried to consider what their other options were. Could they be retained?

## ROMAN CATHOLIC CHURCH AND ITS RIVALS

The Roman Catholic Church had no interest in building relationships with the English colonies to the south for several reasons. Firstly, the French Canadians had received from their new colonial master the core privileges the Church wanted; indeed, she had acquired direct bargaining power on their behalf. Secondly, they saw the Huguenots who, after being rejected in New France, emigrated to the south and were supporting the cause of the English colonies there. The Roman Catholic Church was committed to protecting its flock and guarding against all other religious heretics. Thirdly, in the same line of thinking, there had been spiritual revivals going on among English Protestant churches. Thousands of people were swept up into a spiritual movement known as Revivalism.[112] Protestant preachers became very influential. This engendered uncertainty, because whole cities and villages were being transformed and Protestant churches were started all through the English colonies. Quebec's clergy had too much to lose if they would join hands with the south; wouldn't they be risking religious assimilation by the vigorous Protestant faith?

Fourthly, the Church knew Quebec had been the key target for English colonial invaders from the south, with six attempts made so far.[113] They feared the possibility of another invasion; perhaps the devil they knew (England) was better than the devil they didn't know. Also, in the same vein, the Church was suspicious of people who longed for independence from the monarchy.

That kind of republican ambition was emerging in France also, and the agitators were anti-clerical and secular—against the Roman Catholic Church in France and its power structures that were demonstrating more interest in earthly than religious matters. Such suspicion was well founded; within a generation, revolution would break out in both the American colonies and France, where it would be horribly bloody. The Church in Quebec was relieved that the French Canadians had not been infected yet by this spirit of revolt. New France's clergy did not need any immigrants infected with the seditious spirit of revolution. Such rebels would contaminate French Canadians, and this would serve the cause of the few Quebec patriots who were already resisting the Roman Church's strength over the people.

Finally, Quebec isolated itself from the English colonies because of the long-standing rivalries over the business of furs and the allegiance of the Indian tribes. How could the French suddenly trust them at this time of change and uncertainty?

## BRITISH CONQUEROR'S NIGHTMARE

In 1764, British governor James Murray made a decision concerning the situation in Canada. He concluded the French Catholic society was worthy of Britain's encouragement and favour.

> No military government was ever conducted with more disinterestedness and more moderation than this has been. Hitherto it has not been easy to satisfy a Conquering army, a conquered people, and a set of merchants who have resorted to a Country where there is no money, who think themselves superior in rank and fortune to the soldier and the Canadians (French).[114]

Despite this new gentility towards Quebec, the British government was firmly unsympathetic to the revolutionary movement in the colonies to the south. It was becoming a powerful threat.

The Roman Catholic clergy felt the same way. The *Patriotes*, French activists who were showing signs of insubordination toward the new status quo under Britain and the clergy, were an emerging phenomenon that would require the Church's attention. Understanding this dynamic, the Church adroitly used the situation to augment its power as the middleman negotiating with the British authority on behalf of the French. The clergy were confident they could guarantee political stability; the British were willing to return the favour by allowing the clergy to provide high profile leadership in the parishes, the most significant social units touching the French settlers. At least, England seemed to reason, we can keep the Quebec colony in North America, and perhaps we should make it as large as possible, given the unrest in our English colonies! And the Roman Catholic Church found advantage in the strengthened security available to its people as they invested into an ever-loyal partnership with England.

The American Revolution became a common threat for both the Roman Catholic Church and the British government. They astutely recognized a symbiotic opportunity to protect each other's interests. A working partnership developed and solidified from this crisis. It was a significant arrangement—Canada would continue to be built on the basis of it.

### The Quebec Act, 1774, a Response to the American Threat

In 1764, Governor Murray felt justified in squarely blaming the English soldiers for abusing their conqueror's authority over the French Canadians. For example, immediately after 1760, to qualify for good jobs, French Canadians, through a public statement called "*le Serment du Test*," had to personally deny their obedience to the pope, the Roman Catholic doctrine of transubstantiation[115] and the practice of devotion to the saints and Mary. "Not even one French Canadian agreed to deny faith in the Catholic Church. So they were disqualified from good jobs."[116] The initial British strategy to assimilate the French Canadians included forbidding their French language, laws and customs; this approach created high tension and proved to be unworkable.

Such unkindness toward the French Canadians led Governor Murray to urge the British government to slow down the process of assimilating them, even if it meant giving them unusual privileges. With the lack of manpower, the absence of French Protestants and the encouragement of General Carleton's open spirit to the French, Governor Murray modified the *Serment du Test* requirements. Thereafter, French Canadians could get jobs, including some good positions. Murray and the British government needed more than ever their partnership, considering the strengthening signals of an impending American Revolution. The survival of French Canadian culture and ethnicity was not really a matter of British magnanimity.[117] Instead, the circumstances of the American Revolution and the will of the French Canadians to survive were the main ingredients.

106

British Governor Murray was having his own troubles, as the minority of English merchants—"the Licentious Fanatics trading here"—grew more powerful and troublesome. Though a small number of them had been born in the American colonies, most had spent some time there and had become infected with an unruly spirit of independence as well as anti-French sentiment.[118]

They succeeded in unseating him in 1768.

By 1774, it became evident to Murray's successor, Guy Carleton, that Quebec should be allowed to flourish as a French society of now more than 100,000 people. With apparent generosity, land in what is now Ontario and the rich Ohio Valley were made part of Quebec by the Quebec Act.[119] The land would be safer as part of Quebec than left to the Natives, given the expansionism of the dynamic American colonies.

This move stabilized Britain's political position in Quebec. On the other side of the bargaining table, the Roman Catholic priests were enjoying the influence they had learned to wield, but they seemed nervous over the continuing threat of religious assimilation. The French clergy kept their eyes keenly fixed on the affairs of their colony. How could it be different? Survival was at stake.

The new Canadian blended family had started out with stress. Pierre du Calvet, who heard 3,700 complaints, mentioned that "in one month of English occupation there were more cases to debate than in one century and a half under French occupation."[120]

> All agree that there were some difficulties in the beginning, and that a few cantankerous British wanted to persecute the Canadians and assimilate them. But the Canadians are told that, thanks to the cleverness of their religious and political leaders and their own outrage, they finally overcame all the bad consequences of a foreign domination.[121]

The Act of 1774 granted the French Canadians freedom of Roman Catholic religion, civic rules and language and access to public jobs without "*le Serment du Test.*" Carleton was soon convinced that one could never hope to submerge these new French citizens in a flood of British immigrants.[122] It was clearly best to work with them and gain their co-operation. The table was set for negotiations and mutual compromises; the English colonies of the south were watching.

## ENGLISH AMERICANS ANGRY WITH FRENCH CANADIANS

The French Canadians of New France and the English of New England had been natural and long-term rivals. The Conquest did not help to improve the relationship. Mason Wade wrote:

> At the 1760 Conquest, in this age of ruthless oppression of conquered people, the peaceful transition of Quebec from French to British rule is remarkable and noteworthy. The English conquest might well have meant the end of French Canada as a cultural unit in North America."[123]

Although Canada was governed by martial law from 1760-64, the Quebec Act of 1774 gave French Canadians almost all they wanted, declared Duclos.[124] In fact, the military governments of Murray at Quebec were all too tender to the French Canadians, at least in the mind of His Majesty's "old subjects" who came flocking from Britain and the American colonies to exploit the Conquest. They questioned the British conqueror's negotiation with the French clergy and their making such compromises. The English colonies who also had been mistreated and neglected by the British government perceived in this generosity one more reason to rebel against their English parent.[125]

Once again, Quebec became the target for invasion. In 1775, English colonial General Montgomery moved to capture Quebec militarily. A British flotilla intervened in time to protect the Canadians. Supporting the British authority, during the winter of 1776 Monseigneur Briand announced he would refuse to give sacraments to any local rebels.[126]

Evidently the strong alliance of the Church and Britain had made Quebec invincible to any threat from the south. Though the American colonies were jealous that Canadians had such favour with Britain, they invited the Canadians to team with them against Britain. Even though the invitation sounded interesting, it was laced with dishonesty and egocentricity. Not surprisingly, in each of three opportunities extended by the rebelling colonies to join them, the Canadians remained faithful to the British. The clergy commended the exemplary obedience of their sheep.

## PARTNERSHIP AFFIRMED

The Church, acting as a big sister protecting her French siblings, partnered flawlessly with Britain, who rewarded the Church with privileges such as full control over the parishes and, as we know, the right to collect church taxes. Everyone seemed happy enough with the arrangement. In 1775, Bishop Briand wrote to France that the British authority had no intention of resisting the exercise of the Roman Catholic religion.[127] The clergy cited, when needed, Holy Scriptures to bolster their high authority over the people.

The priests served not only as spiritual guides but also as the local political leaders and community counsellors, so that rural parish churches became the centre of the Canadians' spirituality, culture, community, learning, direction and unity. The parishes were places of refuge but, less positively, ghettos that separated them from many of the realities that would shape the future of their homeland and society. The operative rule seemed to be "Let the English live in the cities and the French Canadians in the parishes." While this approach might stave off assimilation by the English, the price of such isolation would not be cheap over the long haul, as history has since revealed.

Still, we owe the preservation of the French language and culture in Quebec to the Roman Catholic Church. Moreover, "it is in (the) unity of Canadian Catholics' faith, of French Canadians especially, that the Empire will find, in the future as in the past, the most genuine guarantee of its power in Canada."[128] All this gave the Roman Catholic Church a historic role[129]—and a golden opportunity in strengthening its influence—in British North America.

Historian Wade concluded, "Instead the survival of both was assured by legislation adopted a decade after the peace treaty had been signed. The French Canadians benefited from the confusion of British politics from 1760 to 1774."[130]

Indeed, the French in Canada may in large measure owe their survival to the benign effects in Quebec that arose out of the confusion in British politics brought about by the impending American Revolution. If so, perhaps the Conquest, if it had to occur at all, occurred at one of the most favourable times.

## DEPLORABLE STATE OF NEW FRANCE'S ECONOMY

Describing the context prior to the 1760 Conquest, Mason Wade made interesting observations about the French Canadian economy whose

> sole reliance was on fur trade. Agriculture did not prosper and misery was often widespread. Commerce and industry fared as badly; the fur trade passed through its customary cycles of poverty and plenty; while inflation, shipwreck, and the profiteering of French merchants kept the prices of imports high, far beyond the means of most of the colonists...In 1702 it was still the King's view that "The colony is good only as it can be useful to the Kingdom..." Corruption, the shortage of manpower and capital, the difficulties of communication and transportation, and absentee direction all combined to prevent New France from developing a strong and well-round economy.[131]

The weak economy resulting from France's administration of the colony had been a perennial stumbling block to any significant French immigration. As Trudel saw it, a colony needs to offer potential in agriculture, industry and commerce in order to attract immigrants— and this had been not possible throughout New France's history.[132] French Canadians were financially manipulated by numerous opportunist leaders. It was traditionally reported that Intendant Bigot had been the model of organized corruption, taking advantage of the monopolistic situation and the potential for abusing power. "The economic structure of the colony was rotted through by the gigantic swindles of Bigot and his gang of boodlers; division and dissension between Frenchman and French Canadians reigned until the moment of the disaster came"[133] emphasized Wade.

In spite of these poor conditions, as we have already learned, Huguenots had been willing to come to live in New France in order to escape the injustices heaped on them by France and to pursue new opportunities. Quebec offered mostly the same treatment, sadly, and the Huguenots' economic potential was, in large measure, neutralized as they were scattered and assimilated.

In fact, two centuries later, Lionel Groulx wrote that this would negatively affect the colonization. The French population in North America was literally divided into two:

> In 1941, the French population outside of Quebec is 788,006 including 163,934 in New Brunswick, 373,990 in Ontario plus over 2,000,000 French Americans that he called sons of the dispersion. One can affirm that in one century, French population split in two.[134]

The other half of the French population remained in Quebec, which by 1941 was just one province (albeit a major one) of a predominantly English nation. For historian Garneau, political and religious wars were the causes of emigration as powerful as are the issues of poverty and overpopulation today.[135]

The obvious conclusion is that New France's dream to become a self-governing French nation had been aborted largely by the triple faults of the Mother country's neglect, economic weakness and religious struggles, all of which served to hinder the population growth a viable colony needs to experience.

---

108 The word *province* means a British colony in the French context; it has never been changed since. As a result, some nationalists use this meaning to say that *Québécois* are still colonized people.

109 Lacoursière, *Histoire populaire*, p. 462.

110 Wade, *French Canadians*, p. 47.

111 Wade, *French Canadians*, p. 20.

112    Iain H. Murray wrote a book on this subject called *Revival and Revivalism: The Making and Marring of American Evangelism 1750-1858*. It contains 455 pages of testimonies of God transforming lives through the work of revivalists like John Flavel (1630-91), John Wesley (1703-91), Samuel Davies (1723-61), Isaac Bakus (1724-1806), Jonathan Edwards (1703-58) and John Elias (1774-1841).

113    Tessier, *Guide historique de Québec*, p. 19.

114    Wade, *French Canadians*, p. 49.

115    The Roman Catholic doctrine of transubstantiation states that the communion bread and wine miraculously become the real body and blood of Christ during mass.

116    Frégault and Trudel, *Histoire du Canada par les textes*, p. 130.

117    Wade, *French Canadians*, p. 47.

118    Ibid., p. 57.

119    Frégault & Trudel, *Histoire du Canada par les textes*, p. 125. The name *Province of Quebec* replaced the name *Canada* with the 1763 Royal Proclamation.

120    Groulx, *Histoire du Canada français*, p. 45. Quoting Pierre du Calvet.

121    Brunet, *Approaches to Canadian History*, p.96.

122    Frégault and Trudel, *Histoire du Canada par les textes*, p. 137.

123    Wade, *French Canadians*, p. 47.

124    Duclos, *Histoire du protestantisme*, p. 55.

125    Tessier, *Guide historique de Québec*, p. 20.

126    Ibid., p. 186.

127    Frégault and Trudel, *Histoire du Canada par les textes*, p. 149.

128    Lemieux and Montminy, *Catholicisme Québécois*, p. 40.

129    Ibid., p. 35.

130    Wade, *French Canadians*, p. 47.

131    Wade, *French Canadians*, p. 31.

132    Trudel, *Initiation*, p. 145.

133    Wade, *French Canadians*, p. 44.

134    Groulx, *Histoire du Canada français*, p. 312.

135    Garneau, *Histoire du Canada français*, Tome I, p.72.

# CHAPTER 7

# "JE ME SOUVIENS..."

## THE CHURCH TAKING THE BIG SISTER'S ROLE AFTER 1760

❧

*[Counselling in progress...]*

Cr: How are you doing today?

Qc: Better than last time.

Cr: Are you ready for a good session today?

Qc: Oh yes. I guess I need to move on with life. I'm ready.

Cr: Anything special you want to share to start with?

Qc: You might be surprised; as I was reflecting this week, I thought that something good came out of the mess I painted last session.

Cr: Interesting to hear. Tell me about it.

Qc: When we arrived in North America, our challenge was survival. Soon, we learned that to make life work here we needed to be as independent as we could. When you really think about it, what did we lose when France walked away? We still had our faith, and our Church leaders were walking hand in hand with us. Did we need a relationship with a Mother country that was exploitive, allowing her to use us? When we needed something from her, even essentials for living, we just felt like beggars. We never knew if the support would come or not. All things considered, during the time we spent serving our Mother, we did not have an affectionate, affirming parent-child relationship; on the contrary, as soon as we put our feet down here, we felt disconnected, used, devalued, more like a slave might feel, I imagine, serving his master. And we worked so hard at pleasing Mother. *[Sadness on Quebec's face.]*

Cr: What are you feeling today toward your parents?

Qc: Well, I feel our mother sold us to the English and therefore she was of no help to us anymore. The shock of losing our parents produced fear and largely deadened our emotions, I would say, just as a child today may shut down emotionally if her parents are killed in a car crash. Later on, we also heard they were overwhelmed, busy fighting with the mess caused by the French Revolution and other religious and political conflicts. How could things fall apart so much for Mother and her family? I remember Mom's dream about controlling the world economy and her commitment to secure our future. Some "prophets" of the French Revolution declared that France was reaping what she had sown by treating its French children the way she did.

Cr: So, you did not lose all that much, I guess.

Qc: We had so much on our plate. While France was suffering two major calamities during that era—the messy situation within her own borders (culminating in the 1789 Revolution) and the catastrophe of the Conquest (thirty years earlier)—French Canadian leaders were singing the praises of the conqueror, England. As I read for my homework,

> Who could disagree with the unanimous witness of the social upper classes: clergy, business owners, and the property and money set? The clergy would praise the new colonial leaders for their "intention to pursue public happiness and peace." Some of the business class were congratulating themselves for proving to be so virtuous in defeat that they earned the gentle moderation of the conqueror. Several property lords would even dare to write England's king, "We have enjoyed during the era of this civil government such a peace as to make us almost forget our earlier heritage."[136]

Cr: It looks like people were quick to turn over the page on the Mother country.

Qc: Yes. No relationship remained with our parents: they let us down, and they had nothing left to offer us anyway—physically, financially, psychologically and spiritually—but painful memories. As far as we were concerned, Mother had demonstrated little love for her family but lots of interest in material wealth and possessions.

116

Cr: A key moment to move on with life, wasn't it? So, what was the good that came out of the severed relationship?

Qc: It seems that the Conquest finalized the separation of the child and the mother. It was tough to deal with the predicament we found ourselves in. We tried to make some sense of the heritage we were left with— not much to speak of—and we could only turn to the Church, isolated as we were in this initially strange and uncomfortable Protestant, English environment.[137]

Cr: And processing all this was important for you to do?

Qc: Yes. We were like a child still tied to Mom's apron. Finally we realized that Mother had been permanently routed from our home. This is the time we started to call ourselves an orphan. As you probably noticed last session, it was a painful experience in our young lives. But, it's okay! Looking back, I think the Conquest became some sort of a release; we somehow got liberated from what had become an unhealthy, dysfunctional and hurting relationship. From then on, we learned to make life work by ourselves—that is, under the leadership and encouragement of the priests.

## TOWARD SURVIVAL

Cr: So how would you describe the heritage your mother left you?

Qc: For a whole century before the Conquest, we were in a fragile position. Lack of material, financial, economic and military support— you've heard it before. As if that were not enough, Mother failed New France by neglecting to provide academic opportunity. We did not have much school education, and our agriculture provided mostly a dirt-poor subsistence. Many of us were peasant farmers under a *seigneur* [landlord] while others worked for merchants who were profiting handsomely from the lucrative fur monopoly. Of course we had the help of the Church and the priests.

Cr: Nothing from France?

Qc: As I look back on the history of our relationship, Mom continually neglected us until the end in 1759. She served herself by adventurous fur trading instead of fulfilling her parental duties. We did not have much from her to start with, and maybe less at the end.

Cr: After the Conquest, could you turn to your French leaders for help or comfort of some sort? For instance, to your political and military leaders?

Qc: After the 1763 treaty, French Canadians got an eighteen-month period to decide to stay or to sail back to France. All the military, political and other leadership personnel availed themselves of the opportunity to run away from the camp. "Why are they leaving us?" we asked ourselves. "Are they just looking out for their own security? What about *our* security? Or is it because they can no longer make money?"

Cr: That was hard to take, wasn't it?

Qc: It just put a bit more pain in our emotional basket. But you know what, somehow, it was no big surprise. In fact, we realized that most of the intendants, officers and merchants were here in New France for business opportunity, which was all that really mattered to them. But before and after the Conquest, the economy was a disaster and did not offer much for them, unless they practiced corruption. Returning to France to minimize personal loss was next on their agenda. They saw little future under foreign domination. Of course, the ordinary settlers didn't have the option of going back; they had no choice but to stay and submit to the British.[138]

Cr: Their future was uncertain.

Qc: It seemed bleak. The only real leaders of the people weren't from the seigneurial class but were found among the captains of the local volunteer police, or especially among the priests.[139] We trusted the priests. They had been our guides, and faithful partners since the beginning of New France. So many of the other French officials had used or even betrayed us. *Shame on them*!

WELCOME HOME?

Cr: I see. How did things unfold without those who went back?

Qc: English merchants took over the marketplace with good support from the British government. A few French merchants stayed on with no backing, no advantage, no help but themselves. Little businesses died one after another. New France was dying off. Yes...it had to die, didn't it?

Cr: It was hopeless for New France as such. A new identity was taking over.

Qc: Of course! How could it be different? Like I said the other day, thank God we had our Roman Catholic priests to help us keep going.

Cr: In a former conversation, you mentioned that the English children did not really welcome you in the Canadian "foster home."

Qc: That's correct!

Cr: Did you feel this non-welcome from all the English?

Qc: Some enterprising merchants from England and the southern colonies moved in to seize the opportunity for business and profit. As I mentioned before, their attitude seemed to be, "You French kids, you might have been welcome in the family by our parents, but don't think we will let them turn over the family business to you guys! We have worked long and hard to succeed in furs and other commerce, and we jolly well are going to protect what is ours!"

Cr: Did they really mean it?

Qc: Oh yes! A little arrogant smile or a nose in the air—nothing spoken particularly—was enough to betray their pride in being the conqueror's real children with the special status that brings. This is the impression we got: "You do your own thing; but business and the marketplace are *our* inheritance and property!" And you know what? To better guarantee they could control the business and economy, a group of aggressive merchants petitioned the British government to assimilate the French Canadians into the new British society.[140] This did not bode well for our future.

## A Big Sister to Replace Mother

Cr: What was the Church's first reaction after the Conquest?

Qc: We were shocked, of course, to see the Church giving immediate support to the British government. The clergy rushed to establish relationships with the British conqueror. I guess Rome had lots of experience in international politics, though. Under the military regime, the Church continued to manage the French community like a state church,[141] just as she had been doing in France.[142]

Cr: How did it work?

Qc: Care and discretion were the spirit. It was a delicate situation. Bishop Briand and Governor Murray worked well together. Soon, the Church was applauding Britain's governance, but we couldn't understand Rome's unexpected directive: "They must sincerely forget in this regard [referring to being conquered] they are French people."[143]

Cr: Shocking, I suppose?

Qc: It left a sour taste in our mouth. What a statement to hear from the clergy who had been promoting French language and culture for so long! Did the Roman Catholic Church know what she was doing?

Cr: What do you think?

Qc: Rome directed Bishop Briand to publish a flier recommending prayer for the heir of the English throne, that God might graciously protect the faith that he had received through holy baptism.[144] The Protestant baptism was suddenly approved? It was as if Rome advised the bishop to roll out the red carpet to welcome the British conqueror. We heard the Church was given *carte blanche* to become the French Canadians' "ambassador" to the British government. In 1763, Governor Murray reinforced this new relationship with the Church by asking his government to officially confirm Bishop Briand in his ecclesiastic responsibilities; Murray also provided a gift of some financial support to help Briand with his "pastoral ministry." Bishop Briand readily took on the role of *porte-parole* (spokesperson) for French Canadians; he saw an opportunity to strengthen the Church's power in the building of the "new province of Quebec."

Cr: What a shift! Wouldn't this ecclesiastic submission to Britain raise concern among some French Canadians? What would cause the French spiritual leaders to work so closely with English people?

Qc: Neither we nor the Church had much choice! What was left anyway? What options remained? France, as I said earlier, was routed...gone...and in disgrace too, selling us out as she did. Perhaps we could have joined the American rebels, but they seemed more like opportunists who would try to turn the situation to their favour. Somehow, our priests seemed to discern the pitfalls there.

Abandoned, rejected—where do children go when they lose their parents? They turn to the elder sibling; in this case it was our Big Sister.

It was kind of natural for her to take up the role of the mother. The Church was our Big Sister!

Cr: She was willing to play that role?

Qc: *Mais oui!* She acted just like a mother caring for her family. As any maternal figure might do to protect the offspring, she did not wait too long to offer support and respect to the conqueror;[145] he represented a potential partner, of course. It was a strange turn of events to realize that perhaps we were seeing some good will on the part of the British government. Evidently the Roman Catholic Church was longing for a favourable arrangement. That set the table to negotiate a deal. We shook our heads at what resembled a dating relationship between the Roman Catholic clergy and the English government leadership in this post-conquest setting. *[pause, and then with a chuckle of irony]* But then wartime has engendered opportune romances before...that could result in a *mariage de raison*.

Cr: Opportune romance, marriage of convenience?

Qc: The fact that English American colonists were talking about independence extremely troubled the British Empire. The Church saw that Britain needed the French Canadians to keep America, and neither of them wanted these *Canadiens* to join with Americans, who were Protestants. They could engage in a common cause.

Cr: Do you think this clery-conqueror dating relationship worked?

Qc: No doubt. The Roman Catholic Church developed a notable long-term loyalty to the British establishment. This relationship was initiated by the Church[146] and gave birth to a significant partnership. Still, the priests were preaching a sort of double message to the parishioners. It was really confusing for us.

Cr: Can you give some details about the double message you mention?

Qc: Well, after the bishop's negotiation, we could live in our parishes, speak French, live by French civil rules and under the management of the Roman Catholic Church. In return, our priests commanded us to remain under the care and protection of the British government, our enemy, and to cooperate.

Cr: The British were comfortable with this?

Qc: Considering the pressure that English merchants were putting on their government to eliminate French from marketplace and business, the Church had a plan: just stay away from business and the marketplace. The merchants saw little threat in letting us farm and live as French people in our out-of-the-way rural parishes. But the double message lay in the fact that the priests thought that living isolated from the English would protect us French from spiritual contamination by English Protestantism. So they forbade us to have any relationship with the English, to learn English or to attend any English schools of liberal arts and commerce. Instead, we were called to live on the farm and urged to make babies to outnumber the English and grow our parishes.

Cr: So, if I understand well, after the Conquest, you lived isolated from the English?

Qc: Exactly. Smart thinking on the part of the Church. Prior to the Conquest, we had grown to love and commit to our land and the parish life. It had taken generations of trial and error for us to learn about working the soil and developing an agriculture that would fit the rigorous Canadian climate. The priests found the formula that would allow them to maintain the French community in our parish.

Cr: This seems like organizing a state [parish] within a state [Quebec]. Does that remind you of the Huguenots that lived in La Rochelle and were considered "a state in a State" which was unacceptable to Richelieu? Mightn't this be a threat to the unity of the colony? At this time in history, this was an unusual but reasonable accommodation, and ahead of its time, wasn't it?

Qc: It might have been...yes, I suppose it was unusual, but like I said, circumstances were favourable to us. It was an unexpected opportunity in what had seemed to be a hopeless predicament, and Big Sister had found it for us. Of course, her "dating" the British Conqueror was a bit unusual. But it worked. From 1760 to 1960, we French lived this parish lifestyle, mostly in the countryside, but of course there was some urbanization as well. A parish was a lot like family. We learned to survive before 1760 by being "one family, one language, one religion": This new opportunity gave us a shot at continuing to live as we had before, coached of course to live separately from the English. So the Roman Catholic parishes established along the St. Lawrence River remained the fortress of the Church, resisting any real intrusion by the English conqueror.[147] I guess that explains a lot about us, doesn't it?

Cr: [*Pausing deliberately.*] Any other problem relating to English people?

Qc: The priests held us back from knowing, even crossing paths with, the English. These were the same English we fought for centuries in Europe and America—Protestants who are destined to hell because of insubordination to the pope and to the rules of the Catholic Church. We also remembered how they and their religion caused the French family so many troubles in Europe.

Cr: So you listened to the priests?

Qc: They always seemed to know what to do to be safe. Obedience was ours to give. I read in some Protestant missionaries' journals how they witnessed this Catholic spirit of separation from and religious intolerance toward the English.[148] We Catholics saw any Protestant mission as an unwelcome intruder. Let me give you an illustration. Trudel, one of our historians, used to serve mass as altar boy in a convent. He writes,

> When I walked bravely through the early morning darkness, two Ursuline nuns watched over me like guardian angels so when I would pass in front of an old Anglican church I used to speed up because we had been told it was the gate of hell.[149]

Cr: How did you cope with the duplicity by which Big Sister (to use your metaphor) was "dating" the English soldier yet keeping her young siblings totally out of that relationship? Did you talk about it? Did that affect you?

Qc: Well, even though we saw the clergy doing their best to please the conqueror and to act politically correct in public, we knew somehow that they were really on our side, our official spokesmen—*nos porte-paroles officiels et nos ambassadeurs.* As I told you before, Big Sister was the only one who cared enough to believe in us. So probably we felt she knew what she had to do. Maybe, just maybe, she would succeed where Mother had failed. How much we needed someone competent to put some trust in us, to affirm us!

Cr: So you accepted the relationship of the Church with the British?

Qc: We saw its benefits: their ability to negotiate meant we could practice our religion, speak our familiar French language, be ruled by our French civil laws. We were proud of our Big Sister, and everybody thought the outcome was an intervention by God from heaven.

> The priesthood and all the church-going Canadians came to the conclusion that God himself had favoured the British Conquest of Canada in order to protect the Catholic Church of this country and the "nation Canadienne" from the abuses and horror of the wicked revolution [in France].[150]

Cr: Do you believe that?

Qc: Given the facts of our miserable predicament after the Conquest, we just embraced our good fortune. One might say that "the priests played the role of Saviour in the service of our people and boosted our pride as Canadians."[151]

Cr: That's quite a comparison. Priests as Saviour.

Qc: They were our *heroes*! They gave back to us the hope of living after the Conquest took away all hope. They earned our trust. The priests seemed to be omnipresent. Under their leadership, life in the parish had security, stability and comfort. Even though the Conquest made us look like "we were born for little bread," we were content. The Church, our resourceful Big Sister, coached us to take pride in farming and in multiplying our families and parishes, and who knew what the future would hold for us? The dream of a French nation was somehow still alive!

Cr: Well I sense that today you talked about a tragedy of your life that seemed to turn into something positive. Am I right in this?

Qc: *Oui*, I think so. After the horror of the Conquest...*Oh!* Look at the time! I need to stop here. I have another appointment soon. Any homework for next session?

Cr: We will continue here next session. I would like to get an overview of what life was about after Conquest, how that impacted your journey. Can you work on this?

Qc: No problem. See you next week at 7 p.m.

⚜ ────────────────

136   Groulx, *Histoire du Canada français*, p. 17.

137   Lower, *Approaches to Canadian History*, p. 18.

138   Brunet, *Approaches to Canadian History*, p. 85. Quoting Mr. Burt.

139   A.L. Burt, quoted by Groulx, *Histoire du Canada français*, p. 42.

140   Frégault and Trudel, *Histoire du Canada par les textes*, p. 182. The merchants fought aggressively by putting pressure on the British government to take control back.

141   In Europe there is a long tradition of the established church and the state sharing together in the ruling function.

142   Trudel, *Initiation à la Nouvelle France*, p. 115.

143   Groulx, *Histoire du Canada français*, p. 27.

144   Larin, *Brève Histoire*, p. 154. This edict, decreed on January 2nd, 1763, is quoted in M. Brunet's *Les Canadiens après la Conquête: 1759-1775*, p. 38.

145   Groulx, *Histoire du Canada français*, p. 27. Groulx writes, "*Le clergé a pris les devants,*" meaning that the clergy took the lead in co-operating with the conqueror.

146   Groulx, *Histoire du Canada français*, p. 27. Loyally, the Canadians inclined themselves after the example made to them, the clergy showing the way.

147   Groulx, *Histoire du Canada français*, p. 35. Its Roman Catholicism was, for (French) Canada, its first line of strength. That is to say that the first line of resistance of the French colony to the Anglo-Protestant offensive—its *torres vedras*—was its 110 parishes, veritable bastions stretched along the St. Lawrence.

148   For instance, missionary Les Barnhart's biography, *Riding Out the Storm in Quebec: a Biography of Les Barnhart. Bravant la tempête au Québec: Une biographie de Les Barnhart* (New Hamburg: L.G. Barnhart, 1997).

149    Trudel, *Mémoires d'un autre siècle*, p. 64. This was between 1920 and 1930.

150    Brunet, *Approaches to Canadian History*, p. 93.

151    Ibid., p. 97.

# CHAPTER 8

# HISTORICAL INSIGHTS
## SEEDS OF NATIONALISM
## 1760–1960

❧

AFTER THE CONQUEST, THE ROMAN CATHOLIC CHURCH, THEIR FARMS, their language and culture and "making babies" became, for French Canadians, the means to pride and satisfaction in life.

> Their survival was not dependent, however, upon British magnanimity or the forces of circumstances; for French Canada possessed an indomitable will to live, witnessed in the first decade after the conquest by the attainment of the highest birth rate ever recorded for any white people.[152]

ROMAN CATHOLIC EDUCATION

Education was provided in French but at the most basic level. The building of French agricultural communities parish by parish got much more attention. For almost three centuries after the beginning of the colony, post-primary education was not much valued by the Church; she avoided liberal, business or scientific teaching and learning. Duclos wrote,

> For the colonists had been taught during several generations by an authoritarian clergy that did not favour instruction for their people. This produced a mentality that was incapable of progress; for it is almost impossible to introduce any new notion into people's minds.[153]

A few French Canadians were allowed higher education to become priests, lawyers and physicians. They were recruited by the priests, and could not qualify without a letter of recommendation from their priests. Otherwise, "the work of the farm, seasonal mobility and peer pressure caused the boys not to stay too long on school benches."[154] In this context, it was not surprising that women received more schooling than men, which became one step toward developing a *Québécois* matriarchal society. In 2008, it has been well publicized that Quebec boys still drop out of school more prematurely and in bigger numbers and spend less of their lives studying than women, who outnumber them significantly in university.

By 1820, clergy began to express concern about the numbers of students who started to attend anglo-protestant schools to learn English.[155] Missionary Henriette Feller[156] documented the issue. "'You have lived without education very well until now,' the priests would say, 'and you can keep things as they were; it is not worth the risk.'"[157] Ms. Feller suspected that the tension the priests were dealing with came out of their belief that education was the means of French Canadians beginning to read and study the Bible. A certain Doctor Côté of the same era deplored the harmful influence of clergy; he could not believe that religion in which priests keep people in ignorance and in superstition is from God.[158]

Nevertheless, the priests had to be careful, because emigration to the southern colonies was an attractive option to French Canadians. Economic prosperity and more freedom were available there and one could fulfill personal dreams of a better living. But this would happen only if the Roman Catholic "sheep" learned English. The clergy remained vigilant over their flock.

Counterbalancing the paternalism of its shepherding role, the Roman Catholic Church protected the abandoned French orphan from the dangers of scattering and assimilation. Dreams about a French nation sprung up from the scorched soil of the Conquest. Any ethnic group that stops dreaming of some great unifying vision is more or less condemned to die. This was almost the case for French Canadians and even more so for Native people. In the latter case, the society would later come close to death, validating the dictum that "*where there is no vision, the people perish.*"[159]

## AN ATTEMPT TO REGAIN LOST LEVERAGE

In spite of the advantages the conquerors enjoyed, all was not well with Quebec English colonists. The merchants began chafing upon finding themselves a minority: the French far outnumbered them. They were envisioning a province where new immigrants could settle and English settlers would be in the majority. A flow of English settlers, many from pre- to post-Revolution America, brought this vision closer to reality. Meanwhile, the French were unhappy because both government offices and large companies would hire only English-speaking employees for management positions. Dissent in the colony increased until the government yielded to pressure in 1791 and passed the Constitutional Act, which divided Quebec into Upper Canada (now southern Ontario, on the upper St. Lawrence and Great Lakes) and Lower Canada (the portion of Quebec along the lower St. Lawrence), which was essentially New France lands. Each had its own governor, legislative council and elected assembly.

Upper and Lower Canada grew rapidly. In the era of the American Revolution, British Empire Loyalists streamed over into Canada from the new republic to the south, augmenting the population in Quebec's Eastern Townships (*les cantons de l'est*) to the south and east of Montreal, and elsewhere in the two provinces. Not only was their loyalty to England appreciated, their presence in Canada would help the English strengthen the economy as well as their control of the politics in the colony.

During the next five decades, more and more English speakers entered Canada. Attracted less by the British connection (though the religious freedom and political moderation Britain represented were still attractive), those immigrating after the post-Revolution flood had abated were greatly drawn by the abundance of free good land and the opportunity of a new frontier. They flooded in from America, Scotland, England and Ireland as well as from other parts of Europe. By 1840, the English-speaking population had begun to outnumber the French. British strategy had been successful. Today, almost two centuries later, the *Québécois* attempt to survive as a minority group in Canada, numbering 7.2 million people, with 3.83 million knowing French only (53.8 percent), 327,000 knowing English only (4.6 percent), and 2.9 million knowing both French and English (40.8 percent).[160] These numbers suggest that assimilation is a continuing threat to the national dream the French Canadians have guarded in their hearts for four centuries. In the month of February 2008, the headline news announced that Montreal had demographically become mostly anglophone; it is a critical and dramatic point in Quebec history.

For twenty years, dissatisfaction with the situation that developed out of the Constitutional Act simmered. In 1810, Canada's governor general, Sir J.H. Craig, proposed that the British government abolish the constitution and the two provinces be reunited and all of Canada anglicized.[161] This would solve many problems, he believed. Lower Canada's Monseigneur Plessis vigorously opposed this suggestion; since the British wanted to reward the Church for its loyalty and keep peace with the French, the Roman Catholic bishop won his case. This decision had a detrimental effect on the development of the English Eastern Townships in Lower Canada, as immigration shifted to Upper Canada. By 1821, the English were lacking manpower to work all the new farms, and when they asked the government for assistance, the clergy opposed the request because it would help to colonize Protestant lands. The Loyalists and other English settlers already there would encourage any French who settle among them to embrace Protestantism. Knowing how well Huguenots in France had related to England's Protestants, the clergy opposed French Catholics moving to the Eastern Townships for employment.[162] Nevertheless, these English *cantons de l'est* did become instrumental in introducing Protestant and Evangelical faith among the French in Quebec. Still the friction continued.

Through the years it became evident that the 1791 Constitutional Act with its two provinces was not serving the English sufficiently well. The English merchants pressured the British government to take back supervisory roles that had been ceded to the French. While Upper Canada controlled the national economy, that economy was dependent on the *Québécois* in Lower Canada, who controlled St. Lawrence shipping. They charged customs on goods passing through to English ports.

When disagreements arose between the provinces, the French would use these fees as a weapon in their negotiations with the government. This angered the English merchants, and they sought to rectify the situation by gaining the upper hand in political power. In 1822, a petition for the union of the two Canadas was signed by 1,452 English people from Montreal[163] and sent to the British government. In 1828, Britain and Quebec came to a negotiated agreement on customs fees. The proposal to reunite the two provinces was not acted on until 1840. In the meantime, political life was about to warm up in Lower Canada.

## THE PATRIOTE PARTY: IGNITING THE FLAME OF THE FRENCH NATION'S DREAM

Perhaps it was the success of the American colonists in freeing themselves from British rule in 1776 that later fanned into flame the emerging desire of Canadians to seek self-determination from Britain. A new political party, calling themselves *Les Patriotes*,[164] began to grow in influence among the French in the early 1800s. This party heartily promoted democracy, justice and the defence of the rights of the French Canadians, who still constituted the majority group in Canada. For some, this was seen as best obtained within the British regime, while for others, Lower Canada's sovereignty was the preferred means. In this context, any action that was not in line with the Catholic Church's political policy was labelled anti-clerical, which meant "against the clergy's view."[165]

Louis-Joseph Papineau, a key *Patriote* who became their leader, had numerous quarrels with the Roman Catholic Church. His fundamental political views and fiery temperament, combined with his Huguenot roots,[166] resulted in his being a prominent threat to the stability of Lower Canada. His party was regarded as anti-religious; its members were compared to the rebels of the French Revolution. The Church opposed the *Patriotes* as much as they could, which recalls some earlier rejection of the Huguenots. The historic tendency of the French to shoot their own soldiers in situations of disunity emerged again; it was a pattern learned in Europe and transmitted generationally.

In 1834, Papineau led his *Patriote* party to power in the Quebec legislature; the *Patriotes* were elected in a landslide vote, with seventy-seven seats out of eighty-eight and 483,739 francophone votes against 28,278 anglophone votes.[167] His parliament passed the Ninety-Two Resolutions reform bill, engendering a political crisis, in the midst of which the *Patriote* party refused to allow any concession; that displeased the British and their ally, the Church. The English colonists felt they were losing the control over the French population with its numerical superiority. Whenever England curbed one of their parliamentary acts, signs of civil unrest appeared.

Three long years without any answer had passed since the Ninety-Two Resolutions were sent to London. Finally, Lord John Russell's British regime refused the bill. The English resolutely used their authority (that of conqueror and colonial master) to maintain its control of Canadian affairs; they were prepared to take up arms if necessary.

Thereafter the *Patriotes* were divided between co-operation and radical activism. On May 15th, 1837, Papineau delivered a famous public speech in which he called French Canadians not to open rebellion but to a boycott. Later that year, understanding that this crisis could turn into tragedy, Mgr Lartigue, the Roman Catholic bishop, took a public stand in favour of the British Empire. He used (some might say misused) the Bible to condemn any act of civil disobedience, and he encouraged moderation; he quoted the apostle Paul's letter to the Romans, chapter 13, which exhorts Christians to obey civil authority. This text was also supported by a papal decree of *Gregoire XVI*, written in 1832.[168] The rebellion escalated. There were *charivaris* all over Montreal. A *charivari* is a noisy group gathering, ranging from a harmless prank on friends to a public demonstration concerning a person or cause. This was the opportunity the British government was waiting for to jump into the battle.

Fully backed by the Roman Catholic Church, to settle social disorder the British government brought in the army. Police officers resisted and provoked the demonstrators, arresting the *Patriotes*, with imprisonment, hanging and deportation to exile in the United States among the penalties meted out. The trial process left much to be desired; *Patriotes* were declared guilty and punished without criminal trial. Political leadership was withdrawn from the *Patriotes* when, tragically, martial law was declared on December 5th, 1837.

The Church came out victorious in this crisis. Indeed, with the *Patriote* leaders exiled, the clergy systematically regained control over French Canadians, maintaining their unequivocal support of the British authority. There was a vacuum in Quebec's political life after the 1837 rebellion failed; its leaders had been neutralized. There was no other option left for French Canadians but resignation and the sublimation of secular nationalism into religious idealism and pride of rural and parish life; it allowed the Church to renew its authority over French Canadians definitively.[169]

## A QUEBEC WINDOW ON LORD DURHAM'S REPORT

The 1837 uprisings startled the English; so in 1839, they sent Lord Durham to study the problem and make recommendations to the British government. His famous report confirmed that the 1791 Constitutional Act that had divided the colony into the provinces of Upper and Lower Canada was not working well for the English.

Bowing to the businessmen's pressure, Lord Durham recommended that the Constitutional Act and the provinces of Upper and Lower Canada be dissolved. In 1840, the Act of Union was unilaterally passed in England, reuniting the two Canadas into a single province, Canada. This act called for one legislative assembly, which would alter drastically the political process; it would operate with equal representation from the regions of Canada West (formerly Upper Canada) and Canada East (Lower Canada).

This act was as much a failure as the Constitutional Act had been. It was unfair to the French Canadians this time, in that the former Upper Canada bequeathed a large debt to the new government (for which the French in Canada East would have to share some responsibility); as well, the significantly larger population of Canada East was entitled to elect only the same number of representatives as the smaller population of Canada West. In addition, with an equal number of opposing members

133

in the House, a majority vote was impossible whenever the two regions differed on legislative bills. The colonial government was deadlocked too much of the time, coming to a virtual standstill. The next almost thirty years were to be difficult.

Lord Durham had reported extensively on the French-English relationship.

> I believe that tranquility can only be restored by subjecting the Province (of Canada) to the vigorous rule of an English majority; and that the only efficacious government would be that formed by a legislative union...If the population of Upper Canada is rightly estimated at 400,000, the English inhabitants of Lower Canada at 150,000, and the French at 450,000, the union of the two Provinces would not only give a clear English majority, but one which would be increased every year by the influence of English immigration; and I have little doubt that the French, when once placed, by the legitimate course of events and the working of natural causes, in a minority, would abandon their hopes of nationality...The endowments of the Roman Catholic Church in Lower Canada, and the existence of all its present laws, until altered by the united legislature, might be secured by stipulations similar to those adopted in the Union between England and Scotland.[170]

Several recommendations that Lord Durham had included in his 1840 report angered the people of Quebec. For instance, while he stressed the quarrel between English and French Canadians, he then suggested that if Quebec would assimilate into English culture, he believed they would be healed of their "sense of inferiority," and many problems could be averted.[171] Durham is also known for his remarkably sour statement: "French Canadians have no history." This demonstrates an inadequate perception of the depth of French pride in their culture and their deep, sacred commitment to the Roman Catholic faith. The prominent facade of the Quebec Parliament Building depicts the history of Quebec and Canada. Yves Tessier observed that E.E. Taché, architect of the building, has artfully refuted Lord Durham's infamous statement in the fifteen monuments and sculptures of the facade. It also features Quebec's motto, "*Je me souviens*," which was adopted in 1883. Taché's ingenious response to Durham has set the record straight.[172] In 2008, Quebec City proudly hosted a world-class celebration marking 400 years of their Canadian heritage and culture. In fact, it is a world heritage site. The grown-up orphan has an interesting story to tell.

The Act of Union (1840) brought perhaps two advantages: it prepared the way for a national government over all of Canada, and it strengthened the British commitment to self-government in its colony.

In 1840, Louis Lafontaine, a moderate leader representing Canada East in the Canadian Assembly, recommended that French Canadians give up their dream of what had been Lower Canada becoming an independent nation. Even though he acknowledged the Act of Union's injustice toward Canada East, he did not demand its repeal. He also expressed his willingness to co-operate with everyone in this newly united Canada to seek its general prosperity. He believed democracy and participation in the national government would best protect the essential rights of the French Canadian nation and its cultural and religious institutions, agriculture and civil law.[173]

Mgr Lartigue, bishop of Montreal, called for civil obedience and support of Lafontaine's party. The moderates were in charge. Papineau, just returning from his exile in the United States, opposed the union, strongly disagreeing with Lafontaine's perspective and strategy. Later, in 1910, Quebec's Henri Bourassa delivered a memorable address at the 21st International Eucharistic Congress; there he called on French Canadians to embrace the security of the British Empire. He could see how the unity of French Canadians with the British Empire would assure their continued stability in Canada.

It was during the 1840s that the distinction between French Canadians and English Canadians[174] began to emerge.

## CANADIAN CONFEDERATION, 1867

After the 1840 union of the two Canadas, the English population of Canada surpassed the French numerically. In 1845, historian Garneau noted that this union would anglicize the French and subjugate them to Britain.[175] Another step—and a most significant one that would also favour the English—was a proposal to join all British colonies in North America under one central government, with each having jurisdiction over their local affairs. The Canadian leaders invited Nova Scotia, New Brunswick and Prince Edward Island to join them, though these colonies were planning a union of their own. In 1864 a conference was convened in Quebec City, following an earlier one in Charlottetown, and the Fathers of Confederation drafted the terms for the union. Over the next two years, Nova Scotia and New Brunswick approved the plan while Prince Edward Island decided to remain out.

The American economy was growing. The unstable economic relationship between Britain and the United States brought tension. The fear of another invasion of Canada from the United States, combined with American frustration about commercial transportation on the St. Lawrence River, helped the leaders of that day to pull Canada together. The Fathers of Confederation travelled to London, where the final draft (then called "The British North America Act") was passed by the British government. On July 1, 1867, the French-English colony in North America was officially proclaimed to be the Dominion of Canada, a duly confederated country, which would become the largest geographical member of the British Empire.

The first prime minister was Sir John A. MacDonald, head of Ontario's Conservative party, while Sir Georges-Etienne Cartier, leader of Quebec's Liberal-Conservative Party, became his associate. They worked well together, strengthening the new government and making plans to bring all Canadian territory into the Confederation by promising to lay a "from sea-to-sea" railway. Of its three and a half million people at the time of Canada's birth, only 100,000 lived west of the Great Lakes. Much exploration and settlement remained to be done.

English Canada had been successful in overcoming the French Canadian nationalist wave with both its military and political power and the support of the British imperial connection by the Roman Catholic Church. The result was a young, parliament-governed nation with great potential. The English Canadians were numerous enough to control both national politics and commerce. The French and Native peoples would be governed with some sense of English fair play and justice, but their power would be more or less commensurate with their numerical minorities. English abilities and experience in commerce assured their pre-eminence in that field. Even though the next century would show some political stability, tension would remain: Canada was to witness expressions of racism and intolerance. A long battle about protecting language, culture, rights and traditions would find its place on the Canadian agenda. In the midst of all of these developments, periodic waves of conflict among French, Native and English communities would arise but not be resolved. A complex mixed future was about to unfold for Canada.

## ROOTS OF NATIONALISM

Who are the early fathers of Quebec nationalism? Pierre Bourgault, René Lévesque, Jacques Parizeau and Michel Chartrand were certainly key leaders of recent *Québécois* nationalism; each was gifted in knowing how to capture the momentum whenever the spirit of Quebec independence would break out afresh. But nationalism is not a new spirit in Quebec. Its authentic roots are grounded in the deepest soil of Quebec's history, back in time to New France.

From before 1600 to 1760, French Canadians learned to survive in the rigorous North American environment. The challenge of survival arose from many factors, including agriculture and the task of being self-sufficient in manufacturing because of their isolation. And we have seen how the parish lifestyle involved being separated from the English Protestants. A separatist mindset develops somewhat naturally when separate living is the rule.

With an enemy they scarcely knew, with isolation in rural or urban parishes providing much room for lively imagining, with limited exposure to education, the French Canadians were apt to be one with their neighbours but suspicious of all those who could be identified as outsiders. Parish life fed the dream that these homogeneous *Québécois* were still forming a potential French nation.

The Church, always searching for a way to gain power from the English for the French, promoted two "revenges of the cradle" (this expression actually arose from the baby boom after World War II); these were conceived to eclipse the English (and Protestants) in Quebec by sheer population growth and eventually gain a majority of the representatives in government. The priests instructed French families of their parish to have as many children as they could in a lifetime. They felt entitled to come into a parishioner's home and point the finger at any woman who was not pregnant or carrying a baby in her arms; not surprisingly, for a 200-year period, most Quebec families were huge. Trudel wrote, "A family of eleven children was no exception; families of twelve and more were all around; one used to say that a mother did not accomplish her duty until she had her dozen."[176] The post-World War II generation of parents has witnessed this expectation firsthand. At the beginning of the 20th century, my grandmother, Maria Lemelin, had eighteen pregnancies. My mother, Yvonne, had eight and was ready to have more. My wife, Lorraine, with two children, was above the Quebec average for our time. Things have drastically changed.

Gérard Gosselin, showing an interest in the demography of Quebec, wrote,

> In 1951, 20 percent of children lived in family units of six children and more; these strong family units assured natural socialization of children. Today, we find only 1 percent in such a family environment. The tendency seems to increase toward the only child.[177]

In fact, the cradle strategy has now been rejected *en masse* by postmodern *Québécois*; could their aversion to the historic priestly expectation for large families be a contributing factor to or excuse for Quebec's current inability to repopulate itself naturally? Or could their struggle be with the idea of bringing babies into a messy, polluted, unjust, violent and terrorizing world in which life seems to be increasingly meaningless? Or again, could it be they simply want to enjoy the pleasures of life?

Trudel cites the Church as the motor of nationalism in the 1930s, when its seminaries inspired students to the promotion of Roman

Catholic religion in Quebec.[178] From his own experience and training in seminary, Roman Catholic priest Lucien Vinet observed in 1949 that

> Quebec is just as far removed from a beneficial change in its system of education as it was a century ago at the time of Papineau...They have succeeded in planting in the minds of many French Canadians, especially during the past twenty years, a separatist education which calls for separating Quebec from Confederation.[179]

Such ideas were promoted through seminaries, universities and schools and through the Roman Catholic daily newspaper *Le Devoir*, which was then both nationalist and anti-British.

For English Canadians of the 1960s, the concept of nationalism was a foreign idea and of course a threat they could not understand. For the *Québécois*, the concept has always been present in their heart as a means of survival, related to their identity as survivors. Nationalism in the parish was focused on the protection of the French community and its religion, language and traditions. Historically, it involved a commitment to survival in hostile, perhaps fearful, natural and human environments. With the Roman Catholic clergy fully managing the parishes and with their parishoners somehow enjoying the simple security and satisfaction of farming, French Canadians nourished the feeling of being some sort of French nation-in-the-making. Their centuries-old ethos of separation from English Protestants engendered a let's-stick-together-with-our-own mentality. Separation, separatism, nationalism and sovereignty are ideas that are hard to...well, separate, in the historical Quebec context.

❖ ───────────────

152    Wade, *French Canadians*, p. 47.

153    Duclos, *Histoire du protestantisme*, p. 114.

154    Lemieux and Montminy, *Catholicisme Québécois*, p. 29.

155    Ibid., p. 25.

156    Madame Feller (1800-1868) was an evangelical missionary who devoted a big part of her life to teaching the gospel message of Jesus Christ from the Bible in French Quebec.

157    Cramp, *Madame Feller*, p. 141.

158    Duclos, *Histoire du protestantisme*, p. 129. Dr. Côté was closely related to *Patriotes* and Baptist "Bible–emphasizing" believers.

159    Proverbs 29:18, KJV.

160    Instituts de statistiques, Government of Quebec, 2001 Census of Canada: Quebec (by language), http://www.stat.gouv.qc.ca/regions/lequebec/langue_que/connlangoff20.htm.

161    Frégault and Trudel, *Histoire du Canada*, p. 172.

162    Ibid., p. 180.

163    Ibid., p. 182.

164    The *Patriotes* might have been inspired by Du Clavet, a French Calvinist believer (Huguenot). After he emigrated from New France to England in 1782, he published an essay called "*Libre Appel à la justice de l'état* [A call to State justice]" aiming to propose to Canadians a fair constitutional government. Du Clavet's wisdom appeared to be prophetic, much ahead of his time. Later, Pierre Bédard, known as a strong constitutionalist, became the leader of le *Parti Canadien*, which became the *Patriote* party.

165    Church priority was to support and submit to the British government; its main concern was protecting the privileges it had received from the British in order to retain its position of control.

166    Louis-Joseph Papineau (1786-1871) was the leader of the Canadian Party in 1815. He was known to have strong convictions about democracy, and he rejected the option of using arms to secure French claims. Premier René Lévesque also shared uncompromising convictions about democracy. In 1971, he strongly opposed the FLQ's strategy of using arms to gain Quebec independence.

167    In 1837 Lower Canada's population included 140,000 British, concentrated around Montreal, the Eastern Townships and Quebec City, and

510,000 French Canadians, living in Catholic parishes along the St. Lawrence River. http://www.chez.com/rebellions/.

168    Frégault and Trudel, *Histoire du Canada*, p. 203.

169    Tessier, *Guide historique*, p. 102.

170    C.P. Lucas, *Lord Durham's Report on the Affairs of British North America* (Oxford: Clarendon Press, 1912), pp. 288-299, 303-304, Quebec History, http://www2.marianopolis.edu/quebechistory/docs/durham/4.htm; http://www.tlfq.ulaval.ca/axl/francophonie/Rbritannique_Durham.htm.

171    Frégault and Trudel, *Histoire du Canada*, p. 209.

172    Tessier, *Guide historique*, p.145.

173    Frégault and Trudel, *Histoire du Canada*, p. 216.

174    Lalonde, *Des loups dans la bergerie*, p. 40.

175    Frégault and Trudel, *Histoire du Canada*, p. 240.

176    Marcel Trudel, *Mémoires d'un autre siècle*, p. 36.

177    Gérard Gosselin, *"Le Québec, une société menacée dans ses fondements."* Article written following an address given to the members and guests of the *Population et Avenir* [Population and future] group on April 28, 1999, in Paris. Gosselin was a former MP with the *Parti Québécois* (1976-1981).

178    Trudel, *Mémoires d'un autre siècle*, p. 110.

179    Vinet, *I Was a Priest*, p. 100.

# CHAPTER 9

# "JE ME SOUVIENS..."

## 200 YEARS OF LIVING IN A PARISH
## 1760–1960

⚜

*[Counselling in progress...]*

Cr: Last session ended on a positive note, I think. You shared about the Church's helpful role after the Conquest.

Qc: Yes. Negotiating with the British conqueror resulted in a reasonable deal, and we ended up with some stability and even a glimmer of hope. In fact, the priests were our heroes, earning our trust, because they were the only ones who did not betray us.[180]

Cr: The Church played its hand perfectly.

Qc: Yes. As we sought identity and meaning, the church stepped into the gap, playing the vital Big Sister role for us orphans; she taught us character lessons and virtues, like hard work, obedience and respect for authority. We really owe our lives and our French Canadian community and traditions to her. We felt like starting afresh, a distinct society in the making. The development of the 110 Roman Catholic parishes along the St. Lawrence River was the key reality in that society.

Cr: Tell me about the priests in the parishes.

Qc: Well, as I said earlier, they were our saviours.

Cr: What did they do as your saviours?

Qc: They could stand there for us. So we unreservedly followed them. They supervised the volunteer police in the parish in agreement with the British government; they oversaw hospitals, schools, archives, printing, shops and social work.

Cr: Did you feel okay while giving such wide-ranging trust to them?

Qc: Of course—they were our saviours. Being called to become a priest was an honourable and valued dream. The priest had given us a hope and a future.

Cr: Hope and future...this is where your heart is, isn't it?

Qc: Since we left Europe, we never gave up this dream for a French Catholic nation in North America. But I realize now that life in the parishes under the priests also instilled in us a spirit of nationalism.

Cr: Tell me more about this.

Qc: We lived isolated and separated from the nearby English for two centuries (1760–1960). As a society cut off from the rest of the world, we turned inward and became too introspective.[181] And this was doubly so because the English had no interest in mixing with us. They were too busy developing their businesses and urban culture and us, our parishes.

Cr: Did it work for you? Was it easy to go this way?

Qc: I think so. We had been used to living this way so long that we developed the culture and skills that exactly matched the situation. Agriculture, mass, family, basic education, square dances like we used to have at the *Seigneurie*. It was simple, good and secure.

Cr: *Seigneurie*—that's from the early days of New France.

Qc: Yes, it was the large estate house of the landowner whose land was parcelled out to peasants just as was done in pre-revolutionary France. It shows just how historic Quebec is—our history goes back to feudalism in Europe. *Les seigneuries* did not survive the British Conquest.

## EDUCATION RUN BY THE CHURCH

Cr: I see. You mentioned schools in the parish; what happened with education?

Qc: They were staffed by priests, brothers and nuns. Some young ladies were also given the task of teaching *dans les "rangs de campagne"* (country lanes).[182] No lay person could teach unless commissioned and blessed by the clergy. They taught the farm boys and girls to read, do arithmetic and have some understanding of our history and religious faith. The clergy kept encouraging French Canadians to take pride in farming and to get their third grade in school.

Cr: So just a few years of school, eh?

Qc: Beyond the first few years, school was not valued much; the Church opposed any liberal, business or scientific teaching. Colonization was the top priority, and the boys and men kept busy working in the fields during summer and cutting wood in winter.

Cr: What was your favourite subject in school?

Qc: Recess! [*Quebec and the counsellor laugh.*] I am sure glad I learned to read. And I loved history.

Cr: Did you read books? Since you talk about your faith, did you read the Bible?

Qc: We learned to read off the blackboard, you know. Books were costly and rare. Every single book that came into the school had been approved by the priest.

Cr: So did a Bible get into your school?

Qc: Our nun showed us the one she kept in her desk. But I never got to read it. There were pictures taken from the Bible, I think. Do you know what? I read something shocking that I never knew before. Mme Feller related from her experience the story of how the Huguenots had to put up with a priest who walked from house to house to denounce their schools, entering homes at times to seize the New Testaments they had.[183] And if he heard of parishioners receiving a New Testament, it was even worse for them. The priests feared Huguenots because they were educated to read and believe in the Bible's teaching. And she witnessed the public burning of these Bibles, a regular practice of some priests.[184]

Cr: Did you learn English in school?

Qc: *Hein?* It was enough to learn all those subjects in French. And some of us had only three years to do that! Time was limited—when the weather was nice, they let us out to go and work in the fields. And no, we did not learn to speak any English in the parish or the school. No one knew any English. So no one could teach it, and even if they could, why bother learning English? Only a few thought it could be good, maybe those dreaming of getting a good job in English business.

Cr: Only a few?

Qc: As you know, in every family there are special people, not to say "rebellious." Oh, also there were some French Canadians who converted. For instance, Chiniquy, a Roman Catholic priest, converted to Protestantism, and as soon as he converted French Canadians to Protestantism, English lessons were given to them so they might survive financially.[185]

Cr: Survive?

Qc: Yes. As soon as they became Protestants, they were not welcome anymore in the parish; they were rejected and in other cases forced to move out of the parish to avoid causing spiritual contamination.

Cr: What about higher education?

Qc: I thought about this when I was doing my homework and I surfed the internet and found this. [*Reads from notes.*] In 1789, Monseigneur (Bishop) Hubert opposed the development of a mixed [French Catholic and English Protestant] university. He declared that the French people have no time for that kind of learning because there is still too much work to do in clearing and settling the land. He went on to say that some French Canadians can have good training in seminary, where they do not need to pay as much as they would in a civil (meaning government-sponsored) university.[186]

Cr: How did that affect you?

Qc: The city was an unknown world; we felt unprepared and vulnerable in going there. Only a few exceptional and fortunate young people from the parish would continue on in high school and university. Those who were gifted at study and known to be good Roman Catholics would receive a recommendation from their priests so they could enter higher education. Until just before the Quiet Revolution, there were just three options for French higher education, and they were open only to men: become a priest, a doctor or a lawyer.

Cr: What about the other children who didn't get to go on in education?

Qc: Oh, I have something for you. Let me show you what I wrote out as what the typical *habitant* resumé looks like: "Experience: a faithful servant sending furs to France as a means to survive North America's hard living conditions; expert *coureur de bois*; skilled log house builder and apprentice farmer; speaks French only; highly committed to religiously practising Roman Catholicism; educated to the third grade level; no experience in commercial trades, business or manufacturing. Qualities: hard worker, loyal, obedient, submitted to his religious authority."

Cr: How do you feel about such a resumé?

Qc: What good would this be for the marketplace? No wonder an inferiority complex played havoc with our minds. [*With indignation.*] The French Canadians had been so long deprived of schooling that they did not see its necessity.[187] This didn't do any good for our self-esteem.

[*Quebec looks through the window again and pauses; a long silence ensues.*]

Cr: How did you feel about this educational situation?

Qc: Hard to say—but for sure it was confusing. We were told for so long that happiness was working on the farm and living in the parish; they preached to us, "we are born for little bread." We accepted that and believed that outside the parish there wouldn't be much security. And, the more we learned contentment, the less we thought about this.

## Looking over the Parish's Fence for Jobs: a Window on the City

Cr: What job opportunities were there for you?

Qc: Apart from shoe and textile manufacturing, none, really! We needed to speak English to get a good job in the marketplace. Also, schools of business and commerce were only in English. Besides, we were forbidden to move to the city. Some of us did not even know if they hired French people there.

Cr: It sounds like you had no real option to leave the parish!

Qc: Yes, staying was about the only thing open to us, but things were so tough there that we had to find some new work to do, rather than just survive.

Cr: Do you know if many French Canadians left the parish looking for work?

Qc: Some brave ones began to leave, despite the opposition of the priests. Not knowing English, they were at a disadvantage. A few started to speak out and complain about the parish being a prison that had kept them ignorant and poor. That kind of talking was not welcome at all by the priests.

Cr: A prison, eh?

Qc: The parish had so few options.

Cr: And it was that way outside the parish because you had no English.

Qc: With one exception. In 1832 there was still a little pocket of French merchants attempting to launch a project. *La Maison Canadienne de Commerce* was trying to regenerate the French side of the business. The program at *La Maison* was in response to our lack of French education for jobs that would benefit our French-speaking youth.[188] This project was a wakeup call that caught the *Patriotes*' attention. It garnered no interest among the clergy. Our priests were sure that *La Maison* might even spoil the arrangement the Church had with the English colonial masters—the one that would keep us farming in the parishes!

Cr: How did the English feel about *La Maison de Commerce*?

Qc: Well, it was enough to shock and irritate Governor Durham; in this fresh initiative to improve our situation, he detected the dangerous wind of economic nationalism. Along with the threatening behaviour of the *Patriotes*, *La Maison de Commerce* and the constant pressure of discontented English merchants led Durham to write to the British government a report that was unfavourable to the French Canadians. He noted the struggle between French and English. Indeed, they have been fighting for centuries; one does not need to be a diviner to determine that. His solution was disturbing, however: the British government should assimilate us French once and for all. Listen to what he wrote: "I have little doubt that the French, when once placed in a minority, by the legitimate course of events and the working of natural causes, would abandon their vain hopes of nationality."[189]

Cr: What was the Church's reaction to all this? Were you okay with it?

Qc: The Church was always loyal to the British. At times, we French Canadians were preoccupied with what the Church was doing and not doing, and we got frustrated. Before the Conquest, when we initiated a promising new business idea, it was denied us by France. Now it was denied by Britain because both the Church and the English business owners were holding us back. We were capable of becoming a prosperous French nation living peacefully in North America on a portion of the land. There was plenty of room for this. But together the English and the Church refused to facilitate us entering into the business world, and we couldn't get ahead. No, we didn't feel okay with any of this when we really thought about it. How come *nobody ever trusted us*...We needed a break; we needed a chance.

## The Patriotes 1837: a Fresh Wind of Nationalism

Cr: [*After a thoughtful pause.*] What about the *Patriotes*? Weren't they for you?

Qc: Hmm...I guess I never thought about that. Well, that reminds me of a speech by Papineau, the *Patriotes'* leader; he wanted us to have freedom and to prepare ourselves to get ahead. I guess *Patriotes* were for us, but they looked much more interested in big-picture politics and in focussing on how the power got shared.

Cr: Are you saying they were not able to help you practically?

Qc: Not much. Our backward rural parishes didn't hold much interest for ambitious politicians. We were farmers, practical people who needed a clear plan to get ahead. We didn't get anything out of political rhetoric. As for those *Patriote* guys in Montreal, they were blowing hot air about how it was time to move forward with nationalism while the French economy was finally showing some growth and how we had a good opportunity to take control of the St. Lawrence River shipping as our economic driving force. How would that help us farmers? [*Reflective pause.*]

Cr: So what are you thinking just now?

Qc: Well, looking at the big picture, I can see how Quebec needed more political and economic autonomy. Perhaps the *Patriotes'* ideas on nationalism were okay...somehow ahead of their time, actually. I don't know. Where the Church was satisfied with the status quo, keeping us *habitants* as we always had been, the *Patriotes* had a vision for French Canadians to regain control of the economy and become masters of our own destiny.

Cr: You mentioned that the *Patriotes* soon got into trouble with the British government because of their nationalist ambitions.

Qc: Well, neither the Church nor the British government wanted any disorder, but disorderly clashes seemed to be breaking out all over the place. A lot of it was political, but some was religious. The Church was getting nervous with all this unrest, because her longstanding arrangement with Britain appeared to be unravelling. Bishop Lartigue publicly declared that anyone found guilty of civil disobedience would be barred from Church sacraments and would be held responsible and suffer the negative consequences of his actions. And there were both spiritual and military consequences, because the clergy were walking hand in hand with the British officers to neutralize the *Patriotes* in their quest for nationalism (or anyone else who would engage in civil disobedience.) They worked at putting an end to any rebellion. Support from the Church made it possible for the British to put the *Patriotes* into prison, hang some, and deport others.[190]

Cr: How were *Québécois* feeling with this?

Qc: Kind of scared. We did not know all that was going on, because communications were very limited at the time and the great majority of French Canadians were busy farming. It sounds a bit like the same kind of treatment (elimination of those who believe and think differently) that happened in France to Jeanne d'Arc and to the Huguenots. I remember somebody once saying that putting down the *Patriote* uprising might be considered by nationalist *Québécois* as the peak of the plot of the Church with the British government against French Canadians. The *Patriote* newspaper denounced Mgr Lartigue's position and declared him guilty of betrayal of the French Canadian nation. It was well known that Mgr Lartigue went to Quebec City in fear of his life because the *Patriotes* were angry; he finally gave his resignation to Rome in December 1838; he fled the province of Quebec.

Cr: What happened after that?

Qc: This crisis brought a halt to parliamentary activities for about four years. By the time *Patriote* leaders were deported, the Church got another bishop to quickly regain control over French Canadians in the attempt to provide social stability. As I said, we knew very little about all this city political stuff, but we were glad when we heard things got back to normal.

## Conscription: a Dilemma

Cr: Any other issue you found out about?

Qc: I don't know. [*Pauses to search through notebook.*] I don't know which one to bring up. Oh, here's one from much later. I remember the conscription crisis when we resisted sending French Canadian young men to the First World War (1914) and the Second World War (1939).

Cr: You didn't want to lose any young men in war?

Qc: No, we didn't. And especially not in wars that had nothing to do with us *Québécois*. Canada's federal government followed the British Empire and Commonwealth agenda well into the first century after Canada's 1867 confederation. Wars of interest to England of course were of interest to English Canada. The problem was that Canadian involvement would mean recruiting and then conscripting young *Québécois*, whose families had no interest at all in foreign involvement like that. Do you think we would feel like fighting on behalf of our old enemy and conqueror, England, spilling our blood for her? We had the biggest families in all of Canada at that time. We had lots of sons, whose lives would be taken. War is such a bitter experience.

Cr: It sounds as if you weren't about to support the government on this.

QC: No way! Why risk our lives to protect the English over in Europe, or even the English in Canada, who once had considered assimilating us, who had ignored us or discriminated against us for generations and made us French Canadians often feel we were second-class people?

Cr: You haven't had any attachment to them for being unusually fair by allowing you to keep your religion and speak French after the Conquest?

151

Qc: [*Ignoring the counsellor.*] And how could they ask us to risk our lives and the lives of our children, our future, to go to war for France, our delinquent Mother country who rejected and abandoned us? What would make us willing to do that?

Cr: How did the Rest of Canada react to your disinterest in these wars and your opposition to conscription?

Qc: They told us it was worth fighting for freedom, that defending democracy was our sacred trust. They pointed out that Canada was the senior member of the British Empire except for Britain herself. And she was under attack and needed us.

Cr: They were already in the war, weren't they, when the question of conscription came up?

Qc: Yes, and they wanted more soldiers, especially from us.

Cr: Didn't you feel responsible to fight for democracy along with your fellow Canadians?

Qc: What kind of democracy? *"Je me souviens"* the way our Mother country treated us—like white slaves in America. How could we feel much loyalty toward France? You're talking about *democracy*? *"Je me souviens"* the British conqueror that refused to approve the ninety-two resolutions of the *Patriote* Party that were *voted* on *democratically*. How could France and England join together and be on the same side in war when they had fought each other for centuries? *"Je me souviens"* what their instincts for self-protection and defending their own lands drove them to do. Suddenly, they could agree to work together. Why couldn't they do that when we were a new colony in America?

Cr: But that was then, and these wars were quite recent. Don't you think the situation was different by this time?

Qc: What does it matter to us? For the majority of French Canadians, neither of these European wars were worth giving our lives for. We have been manipulated and used enough since we have been in America: first of all, to fight for our Mother country against Indians and English; secondly, for the British Empire against American rebels; thirdly, politically courted by American colonists to join in fighting their enemy, the British Empire...And for what kind of result, for what kind of appreciation? To be used *again*? We are still a conquered people who have been prevented from becoming a French nation when we chose democratically to do so in 1837. And they used arms and martial law against us at other times too. For *them,* democracy is worth defending when it is for *their* homeland and when it suits *their* purpose. I'd better not say more, because I could get very upset.

Cr: Did the Rest of Canada understand and accept your position on conscription?

Qc: Well, they likely didn't understand our position on these wars and our resistance to conscription. This misunderstanding resulted in more anger and bitterness in English Canada toward the French, because they saw us as disloyal and stubborn. I'll just give you an illustration here from my notes:

> Since 1941, major English Canadian newspapers like the *Winnipeg Free Press*, the *Globe and Mail* and the *Ottawa Citizen* were demanding that Quebec get in step (with the rest of Canada). They accused French Canadians of being cowards, traitors, and racists because they refused to fight alongside of English people to defend the mother country.[191]

These war issues stirred up ethnic tension once again between French and English Canada. [*Quebec wipes his forehead and leans forward with head down.*] You know what? I can't handle this right now.

Cr: I see. I think we will stop here today. but you certainly puzzled me just now.

Qc: How so?

Cr: You didn't bring up anything on Canada's Confederation in 1867. Instead you got passionate about conscription.

Qc: Conscription threatened the wellbeing of so many of our families. Loss of life was a real possibility for each boy that would be forced to serve in the military.

Cr: I don't want to get you going on this again.

Qc: Anyway, I did have a note about 1867, but I skipped over it because to us it is only an adjustment, one more way of organizing the

French people and the English people to be together politically in British North America. It didn't make much of an impact on most of us back then, except that there were more English Canadians and provinces for us to deal with than ever before. Other than that, what did it change? I always enjoy St. Jean Baptiste Day[192] more than Canada Day, and most of us have that preference as well.

Cr: All right, if that's how you feel we can leave that as it is.

Qc: That's fine with me, but now I have a question for you.

Cr: Great. Go ahead.

Qc: I know you know your work as a counsellor—this is not the problem—but somehow I don't see where we are going with this. I tell my story, get back into hurting moments, express my feelings, realize how my life has been messy...miserable...Those sessions don't seem to do me much good. Am I missing something here? What do you think?

Cr: I can understand how you might feel that way today. I think your story will come together soon. From the beginning, you mentioned how you were troubled. Part of you wants to stay in the Canadian home, and other days you feel driven to step out of this home, to separate and just live by yourself and for yourself. We still need to get some pieces of the puzzle. Could you find any reason why you feel you are not making progress just now?

Qc: All along we've lived under someone's authority. We have never really made life work out by ourselves, never been fully free to run our lives. Other people have always made the big decisions for us. I still long for real freedom, just as I always have, but, at this point, I am still ambivalent.

Cr: Some pieces of the puzzle are still to come. We need to continue to hear your story. We are not done yet.

QC: How long should this take?

Cr: I have no clear answer on this. Usually it takes time, not just a few sessions, to unveil longstanding behavioural and thought patterns. Something I have learned about counselling—there is no "quick fix." I can affirm you for doing good work in your preparation and readings; I know from experience this effort will reward you sooner or later. Just keep working at it faithfully!

Qc: Okay. I will. What's next?

Cr: It will be about another period of your life: your adolescence and young adult life. You mentioned several times that the Quiet Revolution was a time of major change that turned around your life. Am I correct?

Qc: Yes, during my teen years. As I recall, that period was a great time in my life. On the other hand, it was during that period that I felt recurring and stronger feelings of conflict about our Canadian blended home.

Cr: Interesting. Change has a way of revealing the hidden things that drive us in life. Here is the homework: please make a list of some key relationships you have been in and describe how each has impacted you. This is a good time to write your feelings, okay?

Qc: Yes, I see what you mean. I just hope we can make sense of all that happened to me.

Cr: By the way, did you meet with Donald?

Qc: Not yet. The other day I crossed his path. He said he is busy writing a book on the Canadian home and my story is in it. Can you believe that! But he said he is willing to meet with me soon. In fact, Donald invited me to spend a day at their country place for some outdoor activity.

Cr: Splendid! I encourage you to have a good chat with Donald.

Qc: I am looking forward to that meeting too. When I am finished with my assignment, I will call you for our next appointment. Is that okay?

Cr: Okay. See you then.

COUNSELLOR'S NOTES:

Quebec is preoccupied with protection of his language, traditions and religion. Somehow, life in the parish gave him quite positive feelings and some sense of success, of security.

Quebec started to feel something was going wrong after living a parish lifestyle of isolation and separation for two centuries after Conquest.

Quebec does not quite see yet how seriously he has been limited in the area of education and business learning by living on the farm and in the parish; he has been feeding on a lot of illusions.

Quebec's mind and life focus are totally materialistic. He believes that by resolving his financial and economic situation, life should work better for him. He came to America with this thought in mind: Business in America represented his future. He is still hanging on to that idea.

Quebec has a string of broken, hurting relationships: with his parents–France, the Huguenots, First Nations people, English, American English colonists, Roman Catholic priests, etc. Painful wounds will somehow be resurrected as we keep digging and exposing dysfunctional relationships in his life. When Quebec realizes that most of his relationships have never worked for him, it should reveal the significance of core feelings and help him clarify the things that are going on and hurting badly in his heart. This will hopefully explain the pattern of relating that he has developed through his life until now: insecurity, self-protection, lack of trust, defensiveness and sometimes arrogance.

Quebec is searching for his identity, of course. Where do I belong? Why am I an orphan? Who has any real interest in me? Quebec is looking for affirmation, for someone to believe in him, to invest in him.

Quebec's focus on separation might be justified by his longing to be at peace and to stop suffering in other hurting relationships (his drive for self-protection). On the other hand, his desire to stay in the Canadian home might be a reflection of his deep need to be part of a loving and caring family. Tackle this soon!

Quebec will not grow in maturity if he keeps reacting to the past. Self-pity and feeling like an eternal victim does not help to resolve or to heal. He lives surrounded by other people; he is not isolated on an island or in a desert. It is crucial for Quebec to realize human beings are born for relationships, while isolation produces depression, sometimes suicide. Need to consider emotional healing.

About conscription: a "No!" answer is driven by a deep force inside. Accumulation of crises and wounds tends to transform relationships into power struggles. Quebec is starting to realize that since his arrival in

North America, life has been a series of challenging struggles for survival. He feels like isolating, separating himself. He becomes more aware that broken relationships are now hurting deeply inside.

One danger is that Quebec might be irritated by most of the relationships he enters, getting fed up enough to feel both hurt and desperation. He wants a quick fix, and the temptation might be to search for a scapegoat for his problems (sublimation). His recurrent problems with the English seem to explain his tendency to make the English the cause all his problems and nightmare. Need to take an honest look at what France and the Church did to lead him to where he is and to make sense of what really happened to him. This understanding will be reflected in his thoughts and decisions and the way he relates to others.

We have identified a critical issue. There is a good possibility that making a list of relationships and meeting with Donald will challenge Quebec's thought pattern so that he will understand his life and the people he needs to live with. Let's see what happens.

My own discussions with Donald helped me to understand better some of the background of Quebec and his heritage of broken and painful relationships (cf: copy of Donald's historical insights in my files). Meeting with Donald should help Quebec to get new insights and a fresh look at his problem from a different window. Donald has a different approach that might challenge Quebec's self-pity and victim complex (what Quebec expresses as "I am a loser") and help him as well to move on afresh with life.

❧ ————————————————

180    Brunet, *Approaches to Canadian History*, p. 93. "One must always remember that the ecclesiastic administrators, whose influence was now very great in a society deprived of...natural...leaders, became the most faithful supporters of the British domination immediately after the Conquest."

181    Lower, *Approaches to Canadian History*, p. 18.

182    My aunt Noëlla Avoine (eighty), my mother's sister, taught in *le rang Manitoba*, part of Ste Perpétue parish, *comté* Lislet, (situated about one hour south of Lislet-sur-Mer, Quebec).

183    Cramp, *Madame Feller*, p. 141.

184    Ibid., p. 185.

185    Richard Lougheed, *La Conversion Controversée de Charles Chiuniquy: prêtre catholique devenu protestant*, p. 20.

186    Frégault and Trudel, *Histoire du Canada*, pp. 157-158.

187    Ibid., pp. 224-225.

188    Ibid., pp. 190-191.

189    C.P. Lucas, *Lord Durham's Report on the Affairs of British North America* (Oxford: Clarendon Press, 1912), pp. 288-299, 303-304, http://www2.marianopolis.edu/quebechistory/docs/durham/4.htm;

http://www.tlfq.ulaval.ca/axl/francophonie/Rbritannique_Durham.htm.

190    Frégault and Trudel, *Histoire du Canada*, p. 203. In October of 1837, Mgr Lartigue took a public stand in favour of the British Empire. Using the Word of God (the Bible) manipulatively, he sought to gain more authority to condemn any act of civil disobedience by quoting Romans 13, which exhorts believers to obey civil authority. *Patriotes* were condemned publicly without a criminal trial.

191    Vastel, *Trudeau*, p. 41.

192    St. Jean Baptiste Day has now been changed by the *Parti Québécois* government to the *Fête nationale des Québécois*.

# CHAPTER 10

# HISTORICAL INSIGHTS

## QUEBEC'S AWAKENING AFTER 1960

FLEUR DE LYS

FOR GENERATIONS FRENCH CANADIANS LIVED IN THEIR PARISHES, somehow isolated from their Native and English compatriots and also the world beyond Quebec and Canada. Many *Québécois* were not satisfied with their life. Then, prior to the Quiet Revolution, parishioners started moving to live in the city; they formed the manpower of the province's progressive manufacturing companies. Most of them were owned by Anglophones. They favoured English people in management, usually blocking French Canadians from accessing good, decision-making positions. Some radical nationalists decided it was time for action. The yet-unknown FLQ (*Le Front de Libération du Québec*) would soon be a feared entity in most Canadian households. It would change the course of Quebec and indeed of all Canada. At the same time, the spirit of nationalism increased. Like a boiling subterranean volcano building up to an angry eruption, Quebec was in societal fermentation that would burst forth into *la Révolution Tranquille* (the Quiet Revolution) in 1960.

### TOWARD A SECULAR GOVERNMENT: A MAJOR SHIFT FOR QUEBEC

After the economic depression years (1929-39) and two world wars, the Age of Communication dawned, and it would eventually supersede the Industrial Age. Radio, newspapers, magazines, TV, drama and music invaded French homes in the 1950s. New ideas, new attractions, new appeals bombarded the *Québécois*.

In 1936, a pro-people party—the *Union Nationale*—led by Premier Maurice Duplessis was swept into power, with the partnership of the clergy. Duplessis was a clever politician. During his several terms in office, massive changes took place. He believed it would be easier to change Quebec with lay people than with the clergy, who still held to parish traditions and were against liberal and higher education.

Duplessis appealed to the national pride of the *Québécois* by filling the province with *fleur-de-lis* flags. In the election of 1948, the Quebec flag was omnipresent. He gained powerful influence by handing perks to people in high places, by giving jobs, by quietly supplying favoured government officers with special licence plates that would immunize them from police ticketing, and by building roads, bridges and schools.[193]

By the mid-1950s, the government had supplanted the Church in the role of provider, a task in which the Mother country had so spectacularly failed. Premier Maurice Duplessis'

> most revealing influence has been to exalt the State, to [persuade] the Church to submit, and to exploit the relationship between the two...[in order to] modernize Quebec. He reduced the Church to an absolute state of fiscal dependency for the first time in the history of the province.[194]

He had opened the way for the government of Quebec to play the increasingly popular role of *l'état providence* (the welfare state). The *Québécois* would now go to Duplessis and his deputies for whatever needs and special requests would arise.

## "MAÎTRES CHEZ NOUS"

On June 22, 1960, the Liberal Party, using the slogan *Maîtres chez nous* (masters of our house), was elected to power under Jean Lesage, and the "Quiet Revolution" was on its way. If Duplessis initiated *l'état providence*, Premier Jean Lesage affirmed its role. Step by step, determined to show its "omnipotence" to the *Québécois*, the government started to take over from the Church many of its traditional duties of the past 350 years: governance, education, hospitals, printing and newspapers, community work, care of the poor, handicapped and widows, orphanages, counselling, marriage and birth certification, etc. The government continued this benevolent work with, this time, a secular approach.

There was plenty to be done: *Québécois* were eager to improve their lot and intrigued by their new-found freedom from Church regulation of their lives. The government was generous in its provision and made no demands for religious compliance. "From now on we can count on *l'état providence*," *Québécois* seemed to reason. The Church was gently shown the door out of much of their daily life, reduced eventually to performing religious ceremonies such as weddings, funerals and baptisms and, of course, the ubiquitous daily, weekly and special masses. "We do not need the Church as much as we once did," was the new mindset of Quebec's baby boomers.

### EDUCATION, A TROUBLING DELAY

One area where sweeping changes took place was in education. Premier Lesage declared: "The revenge of cradles is not enough; we need to conquer the brain."[195] The education system was overhauled. Quebec was catching up with the world's industrial revolution; new jobs in cities for Quebecers were multiplying. Rarely until then had any society experienced so many major changes in so little time. The Quiet Revolution was conceived of as a "revolution with a quiet spirit," featuring no violence.

The centuries-old Roman Catholic governance of education had ensured that the progressive economy and modern business were left to the Anglophones, who relished the privileges falling to them out of the inadequate oversight of French Canadian learning. Jacques Parizeau commented,

Heaven is what is essential, we are poor, and we are Catholic and French, and the English exercise crushing economic power over us and are responsible for our subordination and national desolation. This kind of nationalism is essentially negative, and turned toward the past. Its only objective is to keep the order established.[196]

For centuries and generations, this isolationist neglect of developing French Canadians' knowledge and abilities was detrimental. "The Catholic establishment should explain the two centuries of long delay (in social advancement) compared to other western societies."[197] The English kept French Canadians away from good jobs on the dubious issue of language; this would allow them to stay in control of business.

In 1920, 24 percent of Roman Catholic children had completed elementary school. After 1945, 46 percent were getting their grade seven but only 2 percent ever enrolled in grade twelve.[198] Jacques Parizeau was shocked to read that in Montreal in 1946, of 2 million people, less than 500 were francophone bachelor degree holders. Parizeau said in an interview, "We need to understand the *Québécois* had a level of schooling close to Portugal's, among the lowest of the western nations."[199] Until then, the priest in charge of any given parish generally had his "say" over most parishioners' pathways in higher education.

Duplessis' government initiated a huge school and university building program costing $400 million during his fifteen-year tenure; more than 4,100 schools and most hospitals have been built through his mandates, a key step for redeeming the age-old deprivation in schooling. He kept the goodwill of the Church by putting Roman Catholic personnel in charge of new schools and universities, while draining them of real power by shifting the control to a lay (not clergy-controlled) government.

In 1961, the Liberal government made school mandatory until age sixteen and provided students with free textbooks. Several key measures led to the founding of Quebec's *Ministère de l'Éducation* (Ministry of Education). This was a big, albeit quite late, step towards modern education. In 1962, 50 percent of adults twenty-five and over had not completed elementary school sixth grade.[200]

In the 1970s, Premier René Lévesque opened French Catholic schools to Protestant students so they could receive moral instruction, but it was not mandatory for them to receive the Roman Catholic religious teaching. Also, French Protestants were allowed to have their own Protestant teaching; this would lead many of them to attend English Protestant schools. By 1988, a spectacular change had taken place: there were 235,000 university students in Quebec, most of whom were in Montreal.[201] What a radical transformation to move from the lowest level of schooling in countries of white race (next to Portugal) to having more university students per capita in Montreal (around 5 percent) than in any major city in North America!

Education has the same high value attached to it now as farming once did in pre- and post-Conquest parish society. The Quiet Revolution belonged to the baby boomer generation. Commenting on the Quiet Revolution, Parizeau said, "I believe we ensured the modernity of Québec during those years."[202]

## A New Spiritual Wave: Secularization

Premier Duplessis' government also brought significant changes to religious life in Quebec. He persuaded the citizens to trust the lay government just as they had the Church. In a decade and a half, he was instrumental in changing four centuries of culture; indeed, Quebec shifted from a Middle Ages style of governing, in which the Church and monarchy (state) ruled jointly, to lay and secular government. Just before 2000, the *Parti Québécois* government made a radical reorganization again—placing schools in the province under French and English school boards. Then, teaching of Roman Catholic and Protestant doctrine was abolished from the school curriculum in favour of the history of religions, completing the secularization process. This historic decision created much discontent among *Québécois*; some Catholics have been mobilizing and engaging in legal redress.

Quebec experienced dynamic transformation: secularization of education, the splitting asunder of the church-state alliance and the relaxation of its regulation on Roman Catholic society. It was a sea of change for Quebec, with the modernization of work and lifestyle, the blossoming of culture, and *l'état–providence*, the welfare state. Expo '67 and a few years later, the 1976 Olympics, repeatedly showcased lively Montreal and the new Quebec to the world.

### NEW PREACHERS—NEW PULPITS: OMNIPRESENT MESSAGES

Through the radical reforms leading to the Quiet Revolution, the Roman Catholic Church lost its grip on the minds of the people, and many long-faithful Roman Catholics stopped attending mass. Often-imposing church buildings (especially in the cities), once fully filled, began to empty on Sundays, and many were put up for sale, while several others were turned over to cultural purposes.[203] By and large it was a peaceful process, but it was a full-scale revolution as well.

In the generation prior to 1950, the Roman Catholic priest's weekly preaching got the full attention of his French parishioners. Now *Québécois* were exposed to a new set of "preachers" with messages exalting secular values. The pulpit had lost its audience and the confessionals their behavioural regulation of the people. The Church was too busy resisting, or in some cases trying to embrace and adapt to, modernity; she could not navigate purposefully through the tumultuous waves of change. Rather, she was tossed, damaged and lost much of her cargo.

With all the modern voices communicating forcefully with parishioners by way of the media and with the multitude of secularized institutions, people were shocked into insensibility. On their side, any priests who had reasonable discernment came to a frightening realization—that the real "pulpit" in the Quebec community was no longer in the church and that it had a lineup of competing preachers whose messages almost always negated the traditional teaching that the Church and community had always provided and received. "Where are these waves of negative influence coming from? Why are attendance in church decreasing and the *Québécois* asking so many questions? Who are these media talking heads? What does this pluralistic clamour all mean, and how shall we preach in order to maintain good Roman Catholic faith and practise?" they agonized. Their flocks were being scattered much more rapidly and permanently by secularization than the Protestants and evangelicals could have done in centuries!

Quebec opened its doors to the entire world, it seemed, particularly during Expo '67 and the Olympics, but it did so in a much more influential way through opening up to the influx of diverse mass media, the flow of immigrants from all over the world and the democratization and modernization of education.

While for 350 years, Roman Catholic preaching had moulded the values and shaped the French Canadian character and mindset, *Québécois* have been bombarded for almost three post-World War II generations with diverse, powerful messages promoting new or relaxed values and morality, world views from all around the globe, and a new, secular, international, permissive lifestyle. One could hardly imagine any way to turn back the clock.

## ATTEMPT TO MODERNIZE THE CHURCH

In 1962, Pope John XXIII's Vatican II Council in Rome brought great changes to the way Roman Catholics practise their faith, in an attempt to modernize the Church. Perplexed, many *Québécois* listened, but they were relating much more to their politicians and cultural icons than to the priests. Roman Catholics worldwide, those who were older or very attached to traditional Roman Catholicism, tended to be shocked or dismayed by the changes. Beliefs and practices they had understood to be absolute and changeless were being reinterpreted or reapplied or relativized or even abandoned. Others embraced the updating.

But there was a third response, which saddened those who maintained or adapted their faith. Many of the baby boomer generation, seeing confusion on the part of their parents on one hand and being much attuned to the social unrest and rapid change of the 1960s, stepped back from traditional religious observance and enthusiastically marched to the new drumbeats of secular activity and once-forbidden pleasures of life. They, and perhaps some of the priests, understood that "everything was changing" without comprehending that renewal of faith was meant to change them and change their world. In Quebec, the challenge was particularly great because the Church had been so isolated and so unchallenged for centuries. She tried to adjust but too often was left behind in the dust of the tornado of modernism that had touched down on Quebec.

Most *Québécois* loved what was happening—the economic prosperity, good jobs and careers, sexual liberation, growth of feminism, free weekends that did not require church attendance, big entertainment events, freedom of conscience and opinions, and the perpetual seductiveness of the media. While people walked out of the Church, often for the last time, the spirit of the Quiet Revolution ushered them across the porch, down the steps and out to a new pathway for life that was teeming with excitement and novelty.

As the *Québécois* embraced their freedom, many lived it out by becoming post-Catholic and secular. In 1961, 61 percent attended weekly mass, almost 40 percent already having abandoned it; in 1981, 40 percent were attending; by 1984, 31 percent participated in mass, and in 1992, 15.5 percent were attending (10 percent urban, 20 percent rural).[204] Recently, in 2007, a priest I know well indicated that the Roman Catholic Church expects that the 3,000 remaining Roman Catholic churches in Quebec will drop to 1,500 in the next decade. On the other hand, ironically, about 80 percent of *Québécois* retain a kind of cultural allegiance to the Roman Catholic faith; they still knock at the Church's door to get infant baptism and funerals, though for obvious reasons the number of such "Catholics" seeking marriages has decreased.

Yet this Quebec desires deeply to believe in something that could bring fulfillment in life. Where to find it? What about the traditional family? What about old Quebec values like obedience, respect, truth, sacrifice, faithfulness, sense of community? "If it feels good, just do it!" was now their motto. Boomers surfed the waves of freedom and pleasure for almost two generations before they learned to surf the Internet. And the plethora of modern secular preachers (all those being involved in the new media) had their audiences in the palms of their hands.

As a teen runs away from his parents' home looking for freedom, adventure and party time, French Canadians after about 200 years of captivity in the parish had jumped out of the box in just about every way one could imagine. In abandoning their deeply rooted Roman Catholic religion and radically rejecting religious hypocrisy and traditional values, the soul of the *Québécois* was battered, bruised and began bleeding. Could the quest for meaning in life be achieved through nationalism, sports, festivals, nightlife and *bonhomie*, arts and entertainment?

## SPIRITUAL ANARCHY DEVELOPING

The Quiet Revolution provided an open door for the *Québécois* to experience some new spirituality. Quebec's Baby Boomers in particular, and of course their children and grandchildren, have been deeply affected by such a massive change. How can we make a distinction between culture and belief? Too many Catholics have had a negative experience of religion. Who is right—the media or priests? What about the new religions—do they have something we can turn to?

While it may appear that a majority of Canadians and *Québécois* have rejected religion and some have also abandoned God for a while, perhaps they are seeking to fill the spiritual vacuum. In his book *Restless Gods*, Reginald Bibby has some surprising, if not yet obvious, news:

> The findings point to a religious and spiritual renaissance in Canada—new life being added to old life, sometimes within religious groups but often outside of them. There is good reason to believe that the gods are extremely restless. They are stirring in the churches and in the lives of average people across the country.[205]

## WILL CANADIANS AND QUÉBÉCOIS SEARCH FOR GOD AND FIND HIM?

*Québécois* singers and comedians get attention because they sing and talk about personal pain and dying dreams; these messages reflect the *Québécois* experience during the Quiet Revolution. Some advocate, "Eat, drink, and be merry, for tomorrow we die." The race is all about freedom and pleasure. "Let's boogie!" These messages are directed to an ideal of some kind, a quest for the satisfying of a powerful need or motivation. They have a true spiritual dimension, and where they reflect a continued state of unsatisfaction, pain and malaise prevail. As an emotionally wounded orphan longs at the core of his being to find and love his biological parents, many *Québécois* search to connect to some sort of spiri-

167

tuality and greater purpose. Were they searching to meet a God they hope it might be good to know?

## A WINDOW ON QUEBEC NATIONALISM

After living for about two centuries of isolation in their parish, *Québécois* were broadsided by modernity, which brought an unprecedented opportunity to pursue their dream to become or be recognized as a French nation. The Quiet Revolution was a remarkable awakening for them. Will material prosperity and nationalism or nationhood impart meaning and happiness to their lives?

Historians, recording the early days of the colony, were writing history from the window of the patrons who had hired them. Such scenarios lend themselves to the generation of propaganda.[206] Historian Marcel Trudel has cited the Roman Catholic Church's control in the 1940s of the writing, printing and circulation of books through the law of "the index" of permitted books. The clergy watched the publishing enterprise carefully.[207] To write about French Canadian history, one had to be first, French, and second, a practising Roman Catholic.[208] Catholic historian Chanoine Lionel Groulx was building relationships with Protestant historians in Toronto, and this was viewed unfavourably by his fellow priests, who were attempting to draw back one of their straying peers.[209]

In spite of attempts to silence or veil aspects of the past, historians have uncovered fresh primary documents. Their findings have opened a window for new study and publication of Quebec history. In the 1970s, when curriculum was in flux and history studies a target of certain scholars and teachers, some with a nationalist mindset found opportunities to "spin" or interpret Quebec history to favour their view, while others revised it to their federalist window.

After carefully reviewing the French Canadian textbooks (of history), Trudel boldly declared that he was not surprised to see how the teaching of the day helped to produce Quebec separatists.[210] Such statements inflamed separatists. The window of nationalism was one way of looking at Quebec. Nationalism was not very tolerant of the other windows or perspectives on the province. In fact, a common conclusion of the day was "if one is not a Quebec nationalist, one can only be federalist[211] and colonized; in the eyes of many, you are either for Quebec or you must be a federalist." Trudel denounced the judgmental and prejudicial mindset that prevailed during this period of lively nationalism following the Quiet Revolution. Ironically, nationalists had been caught practicing what they blasted the Church for doing for such a long time; times may change, but often people don't!

## PRESIDENT CHARLES DE GAULLE'S HISTORIC VISIT (1967)

As an orphan may seek out his biological parents at some point in his journey, Quebec explored renewing ties with France. Premier Daniel Johnson invited President Charles de Gaulle to Expo '67. During his official visit, de Gaulle regally toured around the province, making eloquent speeches. With many French gathered to hear him in front of Montreal's *Hotel de Ville* (city hall), he nullified any opportunity for reconciliation when he thundered "*Vive le Québec,*" and as the crowd cheered, he immediately followed it with his historic shout, "*Vive le Québec...libre!*" ("Long live free Quebec!").

What a way to taunt his host nation! It looked like provocation. With those four powerful and inflammatory words, during Canada's 100th anniversary celebration, in the heartland of the national feud between separatist nationalists and federalists, he reminded the *Québécois* that the English had conquered them, suggested that they were still in bondage, and skilfully ignored France's failure to protect her child when her enemy was on the attack.

Despite warm applause from thrilled separatists, his outburst displeased other *Québécois*. They noticed his profound lack of sensitivity toward their memory of France's negligence and abandonment of Quebec; had he forgotten France's shameful relinquishing to the hands of the English the whole of their suddenly magnificent Quebec for the fish off the islands of St. Pierre and Miquelon?

And General De Gaulle's clever exclamation profoundly annoyed and hurt the Rest of Canada, who in the optimistic year of Canada's centennial cherished their country from one sea to the other as never before. Many from other provinces who were making their first visit to Quebec were amazed at what they were seeing.

After all, was not "French Canada the first considerable body of an alien race to taste the liberty which is larger than English liberty and is the secret of the modern British commonwealth of nations?"[212] Didn't the British conqueror give the French Canadians the right to keep the language, religion and civil rules they cherished and permission to live peacefully in their Roman Catholic parish communities? Weren't the English Canadians the ones who chose to send their young sons as soldiers to the war in Europe to liberate France from Hitler? Had not the *Québécois* advanced economically at long last, enjoying the benefits of a prosperous Canada? And hadn't Quebec's education, politics, economy and standard of living progressed more under Britain and then within Confederation than under France's detrimental colonial policy?[213]

Perhaps this public display by General De Gaulle was one more of those parental rows in front of a distressed teenager, planting the notion that leaving this troubled home would be the best way to escape the perennial unpleasantness.

In any event, General De Gaulle threw away a historic opportunity to open a new window on New France and her mother's history, to acknowledge pertinent historical truths of vital importance, to ask and receive forgiveness from those whom France had hurt so much, and to get Quebec and France reconciled on a friendly basis.

Who knows how that could have opened the way for reconciliation between English and French Canadians? Instead, ten centuries after the battle between England and France started in Europe, rivalry and pride could still spring up and nourish the roots of bitterness. Perhaps reacting in kind, though with a degree of moderation, Canada declared General De Gaulle's remarks unacceptable, whereupon his visit was cut short and he returned to France.

Expo '67, Canada's delightful centennial birthday celebration and Quebec's spectacular coming-out party, continued for several more weeks, with nearly everyone having a splendid time.

## LE FRONT DE LIBÉRATION DU QUÉBEC: FLQ

For the last forty years of the twentieth century, Quebec claimed itself to be a distinct society. Perhaps it has not unduly bothered

Quebec to be seen as the bad boy of the Canadian blended family as long as he is recognized as distinct from the other children.

In 1960, Quebec's economy was weak. A lot of workers lost their jobs, and too often preference was given to the English when it came to employment. The Quebec government had been inadequate in the fight to erase poverty. A revolutionary mindset arose among politicized radical nationalists who appeared to be some "reincarnation" of the 1837 *Patriote* radicals. The *Front de Libération du Québéc* (FLQ) was a militant group dedicated to Quebec's separation from Canada and independence at any cost. Surely someone needed to take responsibility to clean up the current economic and social mess. Since they looked through the window of the 1760 Conquest, the FLQ radicals identified the English as the root cause of the *Québécois'* nightmares and misfortunes.

The FLQ was committed to fight and willing to murder if need be in order to reach their goals. "We need to take back at any cost all that the English took from us since the 1760 Conquest" was their resolve. The economy was still solidly under the authority of the "English Canadian Establishment," both within and outside Quebec. Exploiting the poverty and frustration caused by a vulnerable economy and the winds of change blowing through Quebec, FLQ radicals efficiently manipulated historical events and insights, in effect persuading the *Québécois* to view the English as the single source of Quebec's predicament.

Mirroring the spirit of 1837's most radical *Patriotes*, who were too impatient to follow the longer pathway of democracy, these *felquistes* were desperate to reach their goal.[214] Impatient for independence through revolution, they began by creating panic through activities that culminated in mailbox bombings, kidnappings and the murder of Pierre Laporte, *Québécois* minister of labour in the Liberal government. As the kidnapping stretched out into the discovery of his murdered body, Canadians, both English and French, were shaken by this atrocity. What could justify such terrorism? How did it take root in peaceful Canada?[215]

## CANADIAN PRIME MINISTER TRUDEAU STEPS INTO THE CRISIS

Pierre Elliott Trudeau had reluctantly joined the federal Liberal party. Indeed, Trudeau's dream to lead a provincial party to build a democratic society in Quebec had failed. "Trudeau bitterly found out that Québec does not need his left wing party anymore," concluded Vastel.[216] This set the theme for his eventual sixteen years of battle with Quebec. Then he led the Liberal party to become Canada's government in 1968.

A scant two years into the Trudeau era, the FLQ crisis broke upon Montreal, Quebec and Canada. A power struggle between Quebec and Ottawa erupted as Prime Minister Trudeau responded to the unprecedented civil violence that shocked the nation.

For the first time since 1760 and 1837, *La Loi des Mesures de Guerre* (The War Measures Act, martial law) was declared by Trudeau. Martial law was a remnant of an earlier age of strict discipline and control of conquered people.[217] On October 16th, 1970, around 450 arrests, 4,600 search-and-seize warrants and 31,700 interrogations in city streets, parishes and villages were executed. A lot of innocent *Québécois* were detained; 90 percent of the 450 taken into custody were released with no charge; they had been arrested without cause.[218] With martial law, Trudeau had obtained full control of Quebec. Under his emergency command, the Royal Canadian Mounted Police made several investigations at the *Parti Québécois* head office, a misuse of their authority.

Ironically, the same Trudeau who much earlier condemned Duplessis for using police oppression to break up the historic strike at the asbestos mine had resorted to similar tactics himself by invoking war measures and the unprecedented abuse of so many innocent *Québécois* by it.

René Lévesque was a charismatic and democratic leader, popular and beloved by the *Québécois*. In the 1970s, he rallied the nationalists to pursue the dream of nationhood. As leader of the *Parti Québécois*, he condemned both the FLQ and Trudeau's response to it. "No one must take advantage of the situation to make Quebec a prison," said Lévesque.[219] Even in this vulnerable context, he publicly affirmed his belief in democracy. On the other hand, said Lévesque with remarkable balance, "Revolution leads nowhere. The only way is democracy." René Lévesque's fair play was evident and his exemplary ethics shone brightly into the darkness of those tragic days.

## RESULTS OF FLQ CRISIS

Part of the heritage the FLQ left to Canadian history had been their success at promoting hatred of the English and federalism. Although a growing number of *Québécois* shared their aversion to the English, they would never approve violence and killing as the means to any end.

By the time of the FLQ crisis, the economy's health had improved, new opportunities were multiplying and the winds of prosperity were favourable. But the *Québécois* had resigned themselves to being satisfied with "little bread" for so long that now the more "bread" they could get, the better. The struggle for independence continued, though FLQ tactics had been discredited. As a result, in each provincial election of that decade, separatist parties gained in the popular vote, until in 1976 Quebec elected *le Parti Québécois*.

Even the more moderate separation-after-referendum concept was a great concern to federalists in Quebec and outside in the Rest of Canada. Following November 15, 1976, fearing Quebec would separate, more than 350 corporate headquarters chose to desert Montreal; as well, 100,000 English Canadians moved out of Quebec as they saw the separatist agenda as likely to be achieved; this was an emotional time for those on both sides of the issue.[220]

The wide gap between Trudeau and the FLQ allowed the democratically committed separatists to carve out some excellent space for a coming era of debate and referendum on Quebec separation from Canada. In 1980, when the *Québécois* were re-electing René Lévesque and his separatist government, Trudeau found one more opportunity to frustrate Quebec: "The paradox is evident; Quebec gave us a mandate in the last federal election."[221]

The stage was set, and Quebec held a referendum on separating to be a sovereign nation. The vote was close but did not succeed. Premier Lévesque accepted the democratic verdict; he offered his co-operation to English Canada to improve the Canadian constitution. Angered at this spirit of collaboration, the king makers of the *Parti Québécois* decided to show him the exit door from leadership. But in 2007, the political parties of Quebec's National Assembly put together a celebration of his unique accomplishments for Quebec on the occasion of the twentieth anniversary of his death. René Lévesque is also highly respected by English Canadians for his respect for democracy; he is the most cherished premier ever in the Province of Québec.

## CANADIAN CONSTITUTION

Pierre Trudeau led the federal government into a constitutional review with the aim of producing a "made in Canada" constitution that would both unite the country and appeal to Quebec. To do this, the British North America Act would have to be augmented and "repatriated" from the United Kingdom to Canada. It was an ambitious undertaking, fraught with the potential for federal-provincial contention and outright failure. Once again, Trudeau set his face to battle a formidable situation.

On the night of November 4th, 1981, now infamous as the "night of the long knives," the non-Quebec provincial premiers, with the complicity of Trudeau and his disciple Jean Chrétien and other federal leaders, settled on a constitutional deal without Quebec's assent. Once more, Quebec was left out. Prime Minister Trudeau and Jean Chrétien left their marks on Canadian history as well as scars on Quebec's back. Lévesque said, "This macabre farce will most certainly go down in history. Never will we accept, in the fibres of our collective being, the effects of such a backstabbing."[222] Trudeau's colleagues reproved him for his arrogance in treating the *Québécois* with contempt even while professing personal satisfaction with the repatriation of the constitution.[223]

The national leadership of Trudeau saw a multitude of controversial quarrels with and provocations against Quebec. His ongoing battle with Quebec seemed to be fuelled by the fact that he had never accepted Quebec's early rejection of him. Michael Vastel goes as far as to write, "Trudeau elevated his obsession with separatism and his need to engage in guerrilla warfare with the *Parti Québécois* above the economic interests of Canada."[224] His sixteen years of re-engineering Canada and contending with Quebec resulted in a complex legacy; perhaps understandably it is somewhat more lauded outside Quebec than inside.

## QUEBEC STRIVES TO FULFILL ITS DREAM

Montreal's Expo '67, and the 1976 Olympic Games provided more employment. Added to this, the expansion of the public service sector in Quebec, including making university education widely accessible, improved Quebec's standard of living and gave the appearance that all was well in Quebec's economy.

Quebec's nationalist governments of the last half of the twentieth century devised elaborate programs to create security, prosperity and a sense of identity. *Québécois* felt the increasing potential for governing themselves with less or no input from federal Canada. Their politicians pointed to a bright future. Surfing on positive financial waves, it seemed the orphan was saying, "Am I not a big boy now, grown up and able to be out on my own?" The confidence and vitality of a strong youth can be impressive.

But there were some interesting cross-currents that tended to skew the trajectory of this surfer's board. Language was one of them. Were the separatists intent on controlling the *Québécois* through language isolation more or less as the Catholic clergy had once isolated people through the parish system? Was the French language to become a kind of parish? And if so, would it be a ghetto?

To preserve its distinct society during the latter part of the twentieth century, Quebec needed to guard its French language and culture in the great English-speaking sea (North America). The *Parti Québécois* government of course valued Quebec being a solid French nation. As parents set rules to protect their teenagers, Quebec's nationalist government decided that legitimate laws to protect its language were desirable. Has French speaking become a holy icon for believers in the nationalist faith? Bill 101 came into being and was greatly welcomed by *Québécois*.[225]

## IS THE SEPARATISTS' DREAM FADING?

Is it apt to see Quebec passing through mid-teens toward adulthood, wanting both independence and his own identity? In 1987, Prime Minister Brian Mulroney, referring to Trudeau's approach to Quebec, the referendum and the constitution, said that there are many wounds that need to be healed and that Quebec needed to be treated with more respect. But Mulroney's new Meech Lake constitutional deal failed after being blocked by Newfoundland premier Clyde Wells and First Nation leader Elijah Harper. Premier of Quebec Robert Bourassa was shocked and upset; he declared, "English Canada must clearly understand that, no matter what is said or done, Quebec is, today and forever, a distinct society that is free and able to assume the control of its destiny and development."[226]

In 1994, Quebec elected Premier Jacques Parizeau, who had promised a referendum (1995). Lucien Bouchard took the leadership of the "*Oui*" camp after the invitation of Jacques Parizeau. The "*Oui*" camp seemed to gain winning momentum but at the end, the campaign was close and the "*Non*" camp won an emotional victory with a very weak majority, 50.56 percent. Parizeau resigned and was immediately replaced by Lucien Bouchard.

*Québécois* continue to be divided into two main camps—federalists and separatists. Their drumbeats are familiar and even stale. What really is at stake in this? Should Quebec pursue autonomy and proud historic identity in its homeland or entry into the global village with its opportunities and rich international relationships? Or can it manage to have both? An added question is, how does the relentless march of generations affect the fortunes of these two visions for Quebec's future?

Premier Lucien Bouchard experienced the tension between the separatists and the slight majority of *Québécois* not favourable to independence; the dividing tension in his party led him to resign. *Le Parti Québécois* chose Bernard Landry, a first wave nationalist, hoping to boost the cause of independence. He promised to call another referendum before 2005 if *Le Parti Québécois* would win the election. Led by Jean Charest, *Le Parti Libéral* won a majority of the seats in the Quebec National Assembly, with 45.9 percent of the popular vote. The *Parti Québécois* got 33.2 percent of the vote. Shortly after the election, Landry stepped down as PQ leader, because he did not get the level of support he demanded from his party through a leadership vote.

The failure of the Meech Lake remedy for the constitutional disappointment, federal leaders' (Trudeau and Jean Chrétien) harsh attitudes, arrogance and continual power struggle toward the *Québécois*,[227] the continual intrusion of the federal government into provincial fields of competency while reserving heavy federal tax space, and the Sponsorship Scandal[228] during Jean Chrétien's Liberal government—all these combined to discredit federalism and democracy among the *Québécois*.

Prime Minister Stephen Harper's Conservative government of Canada introduced a motion regarding the *Québécois* people on November 22, 2006, which was adopted five days later. *"Que cette Chambre reconnaisse que les Québécoises et les Québécois forment une nation au sein d'un Canada uni."* This is Hansard's translation of the motion, which Harper originally delivered in French: "That this House recognizes that the *Québécois* form a nation within a united Canada."

This action salvaged one of the provisions contained in two painstaking attempts by Conservative prime minister Brian Mulroney's government (the Meech Lake and Charlottetown accords, both of which failed) to reconcile with Quebec and rectify the bitterness resulting from the Trudeau repatriation of the constitution in 1981 and especially the "night of the long knives." While Quebec has identified several areas in which the constitution fails to meet its conditions for signing on, the nation or distinct society designation for Quebec and its people was a significant one.

Canada is a complex blended family of ethnic groups of people, in which the people of Quebec are a nation-people with distinct ethnic (historic and cultural) characteristics. Canadians need to acknowledge that among us are found divergent visions of what the sovereign, independent nation of Canada has or should become. The multicultural vision of Canada that celebrates diversity should be comfortable in recognizing some distinct societies or nations within the united country. Another vision of Canada is for its people to forge a new sea-to-sea-to-sea identity, knowing and celebrating the roots of peoples' distinct racial and ethnic origins, while moving ahead to a new, distinct, unified identity as Canadians. This new identity will not be definable in a single race or religious faith or language, however, because the Canadian identity is defined to be pluralistic in these areas. Instead, it will be a matter of some shared historic interaction and values and a common vision under which we try to be unified and fulfilled as we live together, caring and showing respect to our differences.

Is Quebec at a crossroads? The election in 2007 brought a Liberal minority government, a very strong *Action Démocratique* opposition and a decimated *Parti Québécois*, whose leader had immediate pressure to resign. In despair, the PQ called Pauline Marois from retirement. The party felt she might be the best leader they could turn to with her twenty-five years of political experience; she was confirmed in her leadership by acclamation. As a strategy to regain power, she required the party to abandon the idea of referendum in the next *Parti Québécois* platform. A separatist party putting aside a referendum comes across as a somewhat confusing scheme, as the opposing *Libéral* and *Action Démocratique* parties reminded her.

In June 2007, two surveys, one for *La Presse* and one for *Le Devoir*, indicated that 85 percent of *Québécois* believe the sovereignty option has plateaued or decreased since the 1995 referendum.[229] Hélène Buzzetti writes about the results of *l'Association d'Études Canadiennes'* survey made for the newspaper *Le Devoir*: "A great majority of *Québécois*, 83 percent, predict their province will still be part of the federal family in ten years."[230] These results are surprising considering how the Sponsorship Scandal had discredited federalism and democracy.

Is Quebec, the grown-up orphan, still feeling ambivalent? Will he continue to search for identity, affirmation and, above all, a dream for a peaceful, prosperous future? Feeling unsatisfied, *la belle province* is searching for meaning and fulfillment in life.

Where political, financial, social and territorial agreements have failed to resolve ongoing broken relationships among the three founding nations, reconciliation might have a lot to offer. It might help if, and only if, Canadians are willing to genuinely look through this new window. Could this be the next challenge of the several groups of children of the Canadian blended family? Why not?

193   Black, *Maurice Duplessis*, p. 17.

194   Black, *Maurice Duplessis*, pp. 9-10, 60.

195   Lougheed, Peach and Smith, *Histoire du protestantisme au Québec*, p. 35. Quoting Dale Thompson, *Jean Lesage and the Quiet Revolution*, p. 290.

196   Pierre Duchesne, Jacques Parizeau, *Tome I*, p. 106. Duchesne wrote that Parizeau shared the same kind of thinking as found in Denis Monière's quotation.

197   Lemieux and Montminy, *Catholicisme Québécois*, p. 16.

198   Lemieux and Montminy, *Catholicisme Québécois*, p. 46.

199   Ibid., p. 220.

200   Duchesne, *Jacques Parizeau*, p. 217.

201   Lougheed, Peach and Smith, *Histoire du protestantisme au Québec*, p. 35.

202   Duchesne, *Jacques Parizeau*, p. 221.

203   In the parishes, before museums existed, artists needed to use their skills to decorate church buildings and display their artwork, most of the time voluntarily. Catholic buildings possess amazing treasures and masterpieces, a great tourist attraction.

204   Lemieux and Montminy, *Catholicisme Québécois*, p. 67.

205   Reginald W. Bibby, *Restless Gods*, p. 4.

206   Larin, *Brève Histoire*, p. 17. The first historians were Catholic priests, who tended to exaggerate the work of the Catholic Champlain.

207   Duclos, *Histoire du protestantisme*, p. 11. The clergy makes sure the past isn't well known, especially when that past doesn't cast them in an entirely favourable light.

208   Trudel, *Mémoires d'un autre siècle*, p.180.

209   Ibid., p. 176.

210   Trudel, *Mémoires d'un autre siècle*, p. 193.

211   Ibid., p. 232.

212    Brunet, *Approaches to Canadian History*, p. 89. Quoting historian A.L. Burt.

213    Trudel, *Initiation*, p. 223. For historian Trudel, it wasn't until after our integration into the British Empire that we could settle down and live a reasonable peasant's life.

214    FLQ manifesto: Quoted from Francis Simard, *Pour en finir avec octobre* (Montréal: Stanké, 1982), p. 11-15. See http://pages.infinit.net/histoire/manifst_flq.html.

215    "When things don't go our way, we eliminate people that oppose us." Where did FLQ people learn this radical way of resolving problems? Could this be generationally transmitted behaviour?

216    Ibid., p. 87.

217    Wade, *French Canadians*, p. 49.

218    Louis Fournier, *FLQ: l'histoire d'un mouvement clandestin*, p. 340.

219    Ibid., 354.

220    Lougheed, Peach and Smith, *Histoire du protestantisme au Québec*, p. 52.

221    Vastel, *Trudeau*, p. 233.

222    Ibid., p. 259.

223    Ibid., p. 287.

224    Ibid., p. 267, 307.

225    Within that bill was the declaration that French was to be the only language allowed on commercial signs in the province. With few exceptions, the use of English was banned. On the education front, English was to be restricted mostly to those already in the system, their siblings, those temporarily posted in Quebec, or children whose parents had received an English elementary education in the province. (Eventually that regulation was relaxed to allow children of people educated in English in Canada access to English schools.) http://www.cbc.ca/news/background/bill101/.

226    "Meech Lake Accord," http://en.wikipedia.org/wiki/Meech_Lake_Accord#Opposition.

227    Vastel, *Trudeau*, p. 287.

228    The Sponsorship program was created by the Liberal government in 1996 after the near defeat of the federalist side in the 1995 Quebec Referendum. The program was designed to promote federalism in an attempt to fight separatism in that province by advertising at community, cultural and sporting events. Until 1999, it was managed within the Department of Public Works and Government Services. Much of the work was contracted out to private advertising firms. From the program's inception until 2002, sponsorship spending was more than $40 million per annum. In March 2002, *The Globe and Mail* reported on issues with the program which resulted in the Jean Chrétien government asking Auditor-General Sheila Fraser to look into its dealings with a firm called *Groupaction*. In time, she referred the files to the RCMP and began an audit of the entire Sponsorship program. The Auditor-General's report was tabled in February 2004, showing that the government paid more than $110 million to communications agencies for little or no work. New Prime Minister Paul Martin established the Gomery Commission to look into the mismanagement of the program, which had turned into a scandal. The people of Quebec and some other Canadians were incensed at the Sponsorship program itself, and the entire population dismayed by the mismanagement of public money.

229    Hugo Degrandpré, "L'option souverainiste stagne ou régresse, selon 85 pourcent des Québécois," *La presse*, June 23, 2007, p. A2.

230    Hélène Buzetti, "Le projet de pays attendra encore au moins dix ans," *Le Devoir*, June 23-24, 2007, p. A5.

# CHAPTER 11

# OPENING A NEW WINDOW...

## LET'S TALK ABOUT ALL THIS

❧

QUEBEC (QC) IS SPENDING A DAY WITH DONALD (DO) AND LORRAINE (LO).

*[Driving to Donald and Lorraine's Lake]*

Do: Hello, Quebec. How are you doing today?

Qc: I've been looking forward to meeting you again, Donald. And I'm doing fine right now. Thanks for inviting me to your cottage.

Do: Don't we have a perfect day! This is how I like them. Since our quick chat and coffee last time, I thought it would be worthwhile to make today's discussion into an outing. I hope that's okay with you.

Qc: More than okay. I love nature, always have...it settles me somehow.

Do: Let's get your sleeping bag and stuff in the trunk. It's time to seize the day!

*[Quebec and Donald are driving on Highway 15, north of Montreal.]*

Qc: So your wife is okay with my staying over?

Do: Lorraine and I are happy to have you. She's already been relaxing there for a week. We enjoy having a friend with us from time to time. How is your counselling going?

Qc: The counsellor's a decent guy.

Do: You enjoy your sessions?

Qc: Really want to know? [*Quebec recalls in his mind from the last session, "I know you know your work as a counsellor—this is not the problem—*

183

*but somehow I don't see where we are going with this. I tell my story, get back into hurting moments, express my feelings, realize how my life has been messy...miserable...Those sessions don't seem to do me much good. Am I missing something here?"*]

Do: Sure, we should talk about it.

Qc: Last meeting I got kind of tired going over the stuff in my past. I don't see the point. I want to move on. Have you ever felt like this?

Do: Actually, yes. And I hear you. I remember a period I went through; my life was going in circles. I was like a dog chasing his tail as I kept on regurgitating the bad stuff...wondering when and how this would end.

Qc: How long did this funk go on?

Do: Almost three years.

Qc: Oh....

Do: You know what, that's how it might go in counselling too. You might be feeling, what am I doing here? Then one day you click on to how those counselling sessions saved you from getting deeper into the garbage; then you realize that, somehow, you've gotten onto a path of healing.

Qc: Hmm! I hope so...Tell me, how long have you been interested in history?

Do: I wasn't much in the classroom. I went for recess and sports, you know! [*Laughter.*] Believe it or not, I got interested in history when I was forty years old, living in Saskatchewan.

Qc: Saskatchewan? Give me a break—what was over there?

Do: Well, my family and I lived there for three years. Oh, and the fields of wheat, the deer...the ranchers...natives...my college, too. Actually, Saskatchewan was a very good place for me.

Qc: How did you get interested in history?

Do: I was shocked to hear Westerners talking about Quebec the way they did. Their perspective was poles apart from what we saw and learned in school here in Quebec.

Qc: Did you reply to them? [*Slight air of scorn.*]

Do: Well, I was so intrigued that I began to read history. I got interested in it, too. Out there, Lorraine and I had many opportunities to talk

Canadian politics; it was a hot topic. I shared what I learned about French, Native and English Canadians and their conflicts. When Westerners heard my take on history and my story of the grown-up orphan Quebec, "it was eye opening," they said.

Qc: Are you kidding?

Do: No! They said they had never heard this view of Canadian history at school, and that helped them to begin figuring out Quebec.

Qc: Ooooh—the first time I'm hearing English Canadians giving positive words about me! [*Incredulously.*]

Do: It has influenced me, I want you to know. I became more interested in understanding people. Reading history from another focus helped me to grasp other people's values, motivations, dreams, goals.

[*Quebec is getting intrigued by Donald's stay in English Western Canada.*]

Qc: So their history books are different than ours! What were you doing in Saskatchewan, you, a French *Québécois*, living in Western Canada?

Do: I moved there with my family to study. I was thirty-eight; it was a time of transition in my life.

Qc: What a challenge! It certainly takes courage to make such a move. What did you study?

Do: I took two years of a Bible course and worked one more year on a master's degree in family counselling. [*Donald continues the account until his car approaches Boulevard Curé-Labelle on Highway 15 North.*] That was a great adventure for me and my family. Hey, we just crossed Boulevard Curé Labelle. My son, Martin, and his wife, Annabelle, live in the area. Remember the story of the priest, le Curé Labelle?[231] That was a good one, wasn't it?

Qc: Yes, I do. [*Pause.*] As we travel across the province, everywhere we turn we find the names of our heroes on streets, schools, buildings and cities. Everyone with their own story, I guess.

Do: Today we will be driving through Ste-Thérèse, St-Jérôme, Ste-Adèle, St-Sauveur...lots of saints and heroes!

Qc: Your son is married? Fewer are getting married these days....

Do: They are married and have four children.[232]

MARTIN AND ANNABELLE AND THEIR CHILDREN, LAETITIA, FLORENCE, BÉATRICE, ÉLOI

Qc: Wow! This is really boosting the average. I hear it's just one child per home. So, you are grandparents of four?

Do: No, six! Our daughter, Claudiane, and her husband, François, have two boys and another creation in the oven.[233]

FRANÇOIS AND CLAUDIANE AND THEIR CHILDREN LAURENT AND EDGAR

Qc: Wasn't le curé Labelle a promoter of colonization? He'd be proud of them.

Do: You bet! We are proud of them, too, and love them wildly. Family is a great heritage!

Qc: You seem very enthusiastic about your family and that experience in Saskatchewan.

Do: Just loved it. Twenty years later, our children still talk about the great time we had. We have good friends there; some still come to visit. We give them tours of Montreal and Quebec, our treasure cities of French Canadian history. When they leave—and you won't be surprised, of course—they take away a new understanding of Canada's conflicts.

Qc: I don't hear very often about having English people as friends. [*Quebec seems skeptical. Pause.*] Tell me, what do Bible courses and family counselling have to do with Canadian history?

Do: In counselling we learned about people...who they are, what makes them respond and ways to help them develop their character.

Qc: Hmm. Good point. It fits with my counsellor's thinking; he is really committed to studying the story of my life. He says the same things.

Do: He is right. Do you want to hear one story that changed my life?

Qc: Sure.

Do: One day, after one of those emotionally charged student discussions on the relationships among the French, Native and English, we were left with many unanswered questions—in fact, too many! I thought, there must be a way to get past this. I did not understand—it seemed as if a piece was missing in the Canadian puzzle. Walking through the school, I unexpectedly crossed paths with an English student; to my surprise, he spoke to me rudely.

Qc: Why?

Do: He had something against *Québécois*.[234]

Qc: I'm not surprised! [*Quebec keeps making digs like this, seems upset.*] How did you take it? Did you let him know you're proud of being a *Québécois*?

Do: Hmm. Let me say this. I felt attacked, sensed the lack of respect. I struggled with how to reply to this guy. My competitive hockey coach "persona" surfaced right away, but something kept me calm; I felt in my spirit this was a special moment. I listened to him until he had finished. I had learned so much from my new window on things.

Qc: A new window?

Do: I experienced something unusual: *Reconciliation.*

Qc: Wonderful—can you believe this? [*With sarcasm.*] Two Canadian strangers, French and English, meeting in the middle of nowhere in Saskatchewan, and they're going to experience reconciliation!

Do: From that moment, I began to understand that I might have my convictions about our conflict with the English and other Canadians, but I learned I did not have the monopoly on the truth; I saw another side of the story. This moment was a highlight of my journey out west. By the way, this meeting place was very symbolic for me: Caronport is geographically situated right at the very middle of Canada, where Western and Eastern Canada are somehow touching each other. This is the place I learned about reconciliation with this student from British Columbia. I was able to open my eyes on his reality, on his pain. I asked him to forgive us; then, spontaneously, we both broke into tears.

Qc: Interesting timing! What about that English student? [*Quebec still doesn't feel positive toward the English.*]

Do: When we experienced reconciliation, both of us felt special peace and joy filling us. I never felt that before. As a result, we could listen respectfully and with compassion to each other's story and differences.

Qc: I've never heard about that.

Do: This was new to me too. Hey, we are halfway through; what about a coffee? There should be a Timmy's just around this bend!

[*Donald and Quebec stop for a break and line up to buy coffee.*]

Do: It's nice outside—let's take out our coffee. Feel like walking?

Qc: Yes. Let's walk to the park downtown.

[*Walking along.*]

Do: It was smart to build a business close to such a nice park.

[*Donald and Quebec seem to enjoy their day and walk. Quebec wants to pursue the discussion.*]

Qc: Coming back to your experience with that Saskatchewan fellow, what happened afterwards?

Do: The whole scenario provoked my curiosity. Why, 400 years after the foundation of Quebec, are there still conflicts among French, Native and English? How come we interpret the conflicts differently? For instance, most Canadians don't want Quebec to separate, but they see the history of Quebec and Canada as separate stories, almost as if they were two different countries. Two strangers living in the same house.

Qc: It has always been this way. The English have their story, and we have our story. [*Quebec doesn't miss the opportunity to stir up emotion.*]

Do: I wanted to know more, to explore history and find other windows to look through. The more I read and learned, the more the historical insights I collected gave new meaning to Canada's broken relationships. I came to the conclusion that Quebec has the characteristics of an orphan and Canada of a hurting blended family, and this really caught my new English neighbours' attention. I was amazed how much they wanted to hear about it!

Qc: Fascinating...You touch a nerve somehow. [*Silent reflection.*] Donald, I have never heard history this way. I feel honoured and somehow understood.

Do: [*Discerning Quebec still feels hurt, abandoned, alone.*] You know what, Quebec? It's never too late to get a positive start, to build new and trusting relationships. We have to realize that we have good things to share with one another. We are part of the same family, aren't we? And somehow, what I have learned, the treasures I've gathered in life, I want to share with others. So I wrote this story, and it turned out to be rather amazing.

[*Quebec's look changes suddenly. His mind is in turmoil because of the number of hurting relationships he's been experiencing. Yet he feels a glimmer of hope.*]

Qc: I am actually quite happy to have this conversation with you. This is a good day for me.

Do: Glad to know that. This is the kind of conversation I like also.

Qc: How are you doing with your book?

Do: Pretty well. I never thought it would be such a challenge to write a book. It's in the publishing stage now. I am looking forward to getting a copy in my hand. By the way, have you read my historical notes?

Qc: Oh yes. Your stuff actually challenged my thoughts.

Do: Did it help you at all?

Qc: Some of the insights were a shock; it surely helped me to see things differently, but I have some questions for you.

Do: Feel free—ask. We can have extensive discussion today. Anything special you want to start with?

Qc: Reading helped me to identify a lot of my hurting relationships and negative experiences. I was shocked—never really realized how messy my life has been! Do you think I am messed up?

Do: I would say messy or not is not what counts for me. I believe our life stories help us understand what we have become and allow us to find some new direction, and hopefully meaning for life.

Qc: You sound like my counsellor! Sorry to interrupt.

Do: What do you mean?

Qc: He asked me to make a list of my most important relationships from childhood to now and answer this question for each relationship: "What has this relationship accomplished for me?" Your historical insights helped me to do this assignment. The timing was amazing.

Qc: Your perspective, or window as you would say, seems quite different from what I have learned in the parish and in school.

[*Donald stops walking and turns to Quebec.*]

Do: I found that, also. You see the tree on your left?

Qc: Yes.

Do: Walk over to the tree and stand as close as you can.

Qc: Okay. My nose is touching the trunk.

Do: Now, as you stand there, and don't move, give me a description of what you observe.

Qc: I see bark, a big tree trunk. Not much else.

Do: Tell me about the forest.

Qc: Hmm! I get your point. [*Rejoins Donald on the pathway.*]

Do: When you have your nose glued right on your problems, you shut out any vision for hope; then, feeding hurt with self-pity, claiming your rights and engaging in vengeance, you start to regurgitate the hopeless view, the garbage stuff.

Qc: Well, who can tell what I should do? I'm so ambivalent—should I stay in the blended family or leave—it just recycles in a loop, you know.

Do: What's really bothering you?

Qc: Before coming to North America, I felt our French family was always safe and secure, our European home and the backyard were fun places, the French boys and girls enjoyed playing all kinds of games, and sometimes we even had good fun fighting with the neighbours. As soon as we put our feet in America, all we experienced was struggle, defeat—being on the losing side; no wonder many separatists now bitterly call Quebec a "loser"! That's me they're talking about. [*Quebec looks sad, hurt, discouraged.*]

Do: *Oui, c'est la réalité!* They feel frustrated and become angry because they don't get what they are looking for—separation of Quebec. For them, until they get it, Quebec has to be problematic.

Qc: What's your opinion on being *Québécois*?

Do: Well, I am proud to be *Québécois*; I see we are different from other Canadians; we have our own story, expressed in culture, language, values, communities; this is what makes us *une société distincte*. Since the Conquest, Canada has been a blended family. We are reaping today what has been sown by our forefathers, for better and for worse.

Qc: I am glad you mention culture.

Do: I love our culture; I believe culture and traditions should serve us. Something I learned over the years: culture is a nuanced set of values to believe, which become a sort of peer pressure to live by. But some cultures, like some traditions, are good while others may not be. Also, both are changing from generation to generation, sometimes leaving people confused. I don't serve culture, as some people do, as if it were a religion.

Qc: Interesting! I never saw culture this way. But here is a question for you: Don't you feel ambivalent like I do?

Do: With culture, no! With politics, it's different. Especially when we deal with things like that shameful Sponsorship scandal. You saw how emotional it got, probably because it resurrected so much of the past dysfunctional relationship we've had with English Canada for generations. I heard several *Québécois*, strong federalists by the way, who once again felt like leaving Canada. To try to influence our vote with money was disgusting and so dishonourable towards the *Québécois*, and it once again fouled the image of federalism and even worse, of genuine democracy.

Qc: I'll say! Lip service, isn't it. Remember just before the referendum, lots of Canadians drove and flew to Quebec and had this big rally in Montreal. They pulled out this giant Canadian flag and shouted, "Quebec, we love you!" What sort of loving family was this? Act of desperation, I'd call it. This was one more English wound for us. [*Donald discerns that Quebec doesn't miss an opportunity to slam English Canada.*]

Do: No doubt most of them meant well, but such lack of sensitivity hurt me too. For me, though, to stay or to leave the Canadian family is not the point. I have come to believe we are built for a bigger purpose than separating ourselves from Canada would achieve. Although we are a significant distinct society, the reality of today's world is multi-ethnic and interdependent. That doesn't spell separation for me.

Qc: Our French culture is everything we believe and possess. We can't forget where we are coming from and that *we are a distinct society*. It is the one thing they cannot take from us.

Do: What do you mean by "they?"

Qc: The English. They took *everything* away from us...but they will never be able to take *"Je me souviens"* out of our minds, *never!*

Do: After all you know, do you really still believe English took so much from us?

Qc: Anything wrong with believing this? You disagree? [*Quebec's tone of voice sharpens; both pause for a moment.*] They are the cause of our nightmares....

[*Donald allows some silence.*]

Do: Let's put things straight here. You know how we did not have much left from France after the Conquest; our economy was one of bare survival; the few businesses that were starting fell into bankruptcy. It sounds like you've uncritically swallowed the hate-the-English notion promoted by the FLQ activists. Surely you know they've discredited themselves!

Qc: Maybe, maybe not. What I mean is that the English took our land, which had a great potential and was our future. It was the reason why we came to North America!

Do: How could it be different?

Qc: The ancestors of both French and English could have shared the land, a part for each one. There was enough!

Do: If I follow your reasoning, remember that in Europe, France could have shared the land in Europe with the English who once possessed almost half of her land before Jeanne d'Arc engaged in battle against the English. But France won that battle for land and kept it. Why should it be different in North America because we lost the battle? And anyway, don't we *Québécois* still live on our land and hold title to it? Also, don't we remember that the First Nations people possessed the whole of North America before the French and English invaded their territory and took their land by manipulation, alcohol, arms and force? To get a genuine perception of the big picture, we need to move and take our noses off the tree. Don't we?

[*Quebec walks along quietly, seems to be feeling down. Is this embarrassment from being caught in some wrong thinking, or a reflective sadness that opens into change, a transformation of the heart?*]

[*Later, when Donald and Quebec are again driving.*]

Qc: [*Quebec chooses to open up on part of his pain.*] As you know, Donald, I have experienced a lot of broken relationships. Too many...it's depressing. I don't know yet, but I sense your book might be coming at a good time for me. I admit I was shaken up by reading your notes.

Do: Ah...Well, I'll have to expose my soul to you, but I don't mind, actually. There was a time in my life when, everywhere I turned, I experienced pain in relationships. It seemed then that there was always someone to block my goals, my dream. I felt miserable. My book arises out of my personal journey. It includes a precious discovery, actually...more than just learning our history. My book will expose the convictions I have settled on over the last twenty years. Indeed, all I want is to share what I found and now cherish as truth I live by. Don't you share your treasures with others?

Qc: I don't have many treasures left, Donald. The fur, our only treasure besides the land, had to be sent to France. After the English possessed all of North America, we had nothing left for us. Besides, how can you share when you are busy fighting to survive?

[*Quebec is back to expressing resentment toward the English; Donald finds Quebec is regurgitating and decides he can't let him go on like this any longer.*]

Do: Maybe, Quebec, you don't have to fight those old battles. Listen now. Perhaps what I'm going to say will be hard for you to hear. Did you remember how, in part of my story, I just kept on ruminating on the bad stuff of the past...and how it caused me to spin downwards? Today, I've noticed that each time I mention something positive about Western people, you've expressed unbelief and resentment. You actually remind me of that English guy who challenged me as a result of accumulating bitterness in his heart. When one cannot process or, shall we say, emotionally digest an event or a person who hurt you, spilling out the same resentment only produces roots of bitterness that multiply the problem by reinfecting yourself and infecting others. Sure, being hurt is painful, but self-pity and playing the victim role do not solve problems and cannot help you. On the contrary, it multiplies your problem.

Qc: Haven't I the right to be angry? Am I not reacting normally? So, tell me, whose fault was it then?

Do: It would be so easy to accuse France and the Roman Catholic Church; and sure, they were largely responsible for our problems, though we ought to admit they have also given us some things of great value along the way. The point is, blame offers no real solution; besides, it will only divide the *Québécois* more and create additional problems. We've had enough of being divided on the question of staying with or leaving the Canadian blended family. Perhaps without thinking through the consequences, the FLQ chose the English as the scapegoat for all our problems because they owned businesses and were in control of the economy, which is what *Québécois* nationalists were looking for us to do ourselves. This strategy did rally many *Québécois* against English Canadians, while the problems from France and the Roman Catholic Church were overlooked. It was not rare to hear a *Québécois* cursing "*les* _____ *Anglais.*" Now, tell me, did this help to solve our problems? To heal broken relationships?

Qc: [*Quebec feels puzzled...does not know what to answer, although Donald seems committed to helping him along.*] Surely somebody must be responsible for the mess in my life—France... the Church... the English. Oh, I don't know!

Do: What does it accomplish for you to hold someone guilty? What does it accomplish to see yourself as victim again and again, even if someone had taken advantage of you? Does it build you up? Life has much more to offer you than bitter memories. What really matters is not to find who is guilty but to understand what led you into this predicament and find the right way out of it. Otherwise, the malaise will destroy you in time. What matters are people and relationships. Don't you think?

Qc: Like I said, the timing of your book might help me.

[*He reaches for the CD player and turns up the volume. Québécois poet and singer Raymond Lévesque is singing.*] I like this song.

Do: It's a beautiful *Québécois* song. Part of our musical treasure.

*Quand les hommes vivront d'amour; ce sera la paix sur la terre...*
[When men live on love, it will be peace on earth.][235]

[*The men in the car hum and then Quebec sings along, and they continue chatting back and forth about themselves; then they plan the day, just before arriving at Donald and Lorraine's country place.*]

---

231 Le Curé Labelle was a Catholic priest who was given by the government of Quebec the responsibility of colonization of the North of Montreal. He encouraged farming and big families.

232 Twin girls, Laetitia and Florence (five), Béatrice (three) and their boy, Éloi (two).

233 Laurent (three), Edgar (one) and...

234   Read about the rude confrontation in the introduction.

235   Raymond Lévesque, http://www.chansonduquebec.com/.

# CHAPTER 12

# OPENING A NEW WINDOW...

## LIFE WILL WORK, IF...

❖

*[Donald and Quebec arrive at the cottage.]*

Do: Meet my wife, Lorraine.

Lo: Welcome to our home-away-from-home, Quebec.

Qc: Thank you for your invitation.

Lo: How was the drive up?

Qc: With this splendid weather, you couldn't ask for more. We talked all the way, no lack of subject material!

Lo: No doubt. You found the right guy to talk to about history.

Qc: How is your holiday going, Lorraine?

Lo: It's very good. I needed this rest. I'm glad to be out of our busy home for a while. I really appreciate my "Sabbath" week.

Qc: Sabbath? Are you doing this as a religious observance?

Lo: Let me put it this way. I believe that people need to rest from daily work, responsibilities and preoccupations—one day out of seven for physical and spiritual renewal; it is so good to get away from daily routine and business, to rest, read, listen to nature and to God, and recharge my drained batteries! We live in a society that demands we perform. *[Smiles.]* I'm sure you're sorry you asked! I've been journaling on this topic this week.

Qc: *[Laughs.]* Interesting thoughts, anyway. You are right, people are too busy. So you write too?

Lo: Oh, Donald's our writer, but journaling is part of my renewal process.

Do: Quebec and I are thinking of some canoeing.

Lo: Can I offer you a drink, a little snack?

Qc: No thank you. We had one halfway here.

Do: If you want to relax a bit in your room, we can leave in about an hour. Get some Sabbath, my friend!

Qc: I think I will. See, Lorraine, you won me over!

[*Around mid-afternoon, Donald and Quebec are canoeing on the lake.*]

Qc: I feel lucky to be here on such a perfect day. This is the place to be. It's so calm.

Do: What a difference from Montreal, eh?

Qc: I like this Sabbath idea of rest and renewal.

Do: I like it too. There was a time in my life when I never stopped working. For eighteen years, it was ninety hours a week. I wanted success but never was satisfied with whatever I achieved. No time for my wife and for my children. If you wanted a relationship with me, you had to perform or I deleted your file. That was Donald's way then. Can you believe I was so unrelational?

Qc: [*A little uncomfortably.*] I don't want to seem to be regurgitating, but...I am totally determined to make life work for me, and yes, I want to do it my way. Experience confirms I must not trust people! I don't want to waste much time or energy in relationships. They make it so messy....

Do: Look at the duck and her ducklings over there by the shore...they just slide on water; it seems so easy.

Qc: You see how she watches out for them; as soon as she saw us, she led them off in another direction.

Do: Good point, man. Lessons for Quebec from the animal kingdom. Here's another: in nature, mothers care for their offspring until they can go on their own.

Qc: Some humans could learn a lot from the animals! Look at that one, he's still young, but swimming alone by himself. [*Donald is focusing on the parallel with the Mother country who abandoned her French children in the North American wilderness. He wonders if Quebec is also.*]

Do: He is a bit bigger isn't he? He'll make it on his own.

Qc: Simply gorgeous to see them in the wild like this.

[*The canoe is sliding gently through the water while Donald and Quebec take in nature's beauty.*]

Do: So, where are your thoughts now?

Qc: I'm thinking of when I was a little like this lone duck, ready to leave the family and live on my own. For too long others decided for me, thought for me and dreamt for me...with messy results I still seem to be reaping. I was thinking it's better living by myself—on my own, away from troubles, away from predator-type people. I still see it that way. This duck can take care of himself now, take his destiny into his own hands, maybe make something of it!

Do: You have already tried to make life work out for yourself.

Qc: What do you mean?

Do: This is how I see it. Until now you've tried to find happiness and meaning in life by investing in all kind of values and directions. Through different seasons of your life, you thought: Life will work for me—if. Just think of all your "ifs!" you have come to believe through your life experiences. Your mind now suggests that life will work for *me*...

...if I go to America to make my future with the luxury business of fur.

...if I live exclusively in our parish with our French language and Roman Catholic religion.

...if I adopt the changes and the values hawked by the loud modern preachers of the Quiet Revolution.

...if I succeed in state-of-the-art education in a field that really matters, business, for example.

...if we can seize control of our own economy and businesses.

...if a nationalist government is elected and makes changes to suit our demands.

...if the government fulfills all our needs as it calls itself *l'État Providence* [meaning to Quebec, omnipotent, all-powerful].

...and you *chose* to believe each time, life will work *if*....

[*Some silent, reflective canoeing, the sound of paddles splashing and then the call of a loon.*]

Qc: Ah, this was Quebec, *non?*

Do: Yes, and Canada too. They do this up in the north of Saskatchewan, you know!

Qc: So what are you saying about all these *ifs*, Donald?

Do: It has now been almost half a century since breezes of the Quiet Revolution started to influence you and brought significant change to your life. What do you think—are *Québécois* feeling any better? Are they happier surfing on their new wave of freedom?

Qc: Hmm. Many things changed and improved...*but*, don't you think we could still have more freedom?

Do: Of course you could have more freedom, but two questions are screaming for answers. How is life going to work for you? And where are you looking to find meaning in life?

Qc: Let me describe my personal dream. We could become the new world French nation we envisioned when we were New France, an amazing one. Rich, free, creative, classy, different than all our neighbours and probably better. We would have security and community like we once had in the parish, but no religion and no federal English people to interfere with us this time. We would have one mentality and spirit, we'd share in developing our distinct society and live united, as we modelled for so long in our safe and secure parishes.

Do: [*Gently, thoughtfully.*] As you look at your long list of broken relationships, how well might it work out this time? You said you cannot trust anyone now. Even in the *Parti Québécois,* the members knife one another, breaking relationships. Aren't human beings created for relationship?

Qc: If we are created for relationship, after looking at my track record, I'd say the Creator did not do his homework.

Do: In other words it's always someone else's fault?

Qc: Just joking, Donald!

Do: Don't you think you have your own responsibility in all this muddle? Remember, sooner or later, you'll ruin your life by remaining a victim. We ought to take responsibility for our actions and decisions, past, present and future.

Qc: I'm just realizing now how playing the victim role does not resolve our problems. And it's not that easy!

Do: A question, then. How can you live in a parish style again, isolated? How is it going to work?

Qc: I have my idea on this! Have I not the right to dream?

Do: Didn't I hear you say, "No more energy to invest in relationships"? You mentioned your experience proves that all the people who got in relationships with you failed you and hurt you. How can you ensure *Québécois* are trustworthy considering what Mother France, Big Sister's priests and others have done to us? After all, weren't they French people of your own blood? And what about the Huguenots you wanted to do away with?

[*Quebec feels conflicted emotions spinning around in his mind...then he tunes back in to Donald, who finishes up with the following.*]

...Let's be realistic here, Quebec's demography has changed a lot. Better be ready; you are going to have to make a lot of reasonable accommodations. Whether you like it or not, a great challenge is waiting for you; you better be ready!

Qc: What do you mean? I guess there's too much for me to process all at once.

Do: Quebec is multi-ethnic, with so few *Québécois* babies. We survive by immigration; multiculturalism seems irreversible at this point. How would you handle the broken relationships, the hurt and the wounds that would arise from any attempt to separate the English, French, Native and new ethnic children of the rest of our Quebec blended home, let alone the Canadian one? What about the *Québécois* First Nations who want to separate from Quebec along with their lands?...

[*While listening carefully, Quebec stops paddling; his eyes wander toward the young lone duck, which is just a dot on the lake now.*]

...Some of the advocates of our Quiet Revolution have been selling you lots of illusions and giving you their benediction, so to speak, to follow an agenda that focuses on radical social change, maximum pleasure-seeking, dismantling the traditional values, focusing on self-fulfillment...whatever *that* is...even at the expense of the family and community values.

...How will you succeed in building relationships with new immigrants from your heritage of unresolved and broken relationships?

Qc: [*Feeling puzzled.*] I never really saw it this way, and I don't want to now, either. Why should we give up our dream just because of all these other people? We were here 400 years ago, and we wanted to start something very special.

Do: [*Gently, after giving Quebec some space and silence.*] So what are the results, Quebec? Did the business of fur, the 200 years of life in the parish, the freedom and pleasures of the Quiet Revolution and the struggles and advancement of nationalism work out for you, as promised time after time?

Qc: Somehow yes! Somehow no!

Do: I think it is great to be proud of who we are, *Québécois*, a distinct society. But, do you imagine you can fill your emptiness with money, business, career, collecting material possessions, pleasures, sex, drinking, eating, festivals, partying...? Don't you think we are created for more?

[*Quebec neither paddles nor speaks.*]

...If life is meaningless, "let's eat and drink for tomorrow we will die" as the old saying goes;[236] where has this led you?

Qc: Why does it have to lead us anywhere? We can just be happy as we are.

Do: But you know you aren't, and independence won't make much difference to how you feel. If you genuinely examine your life, can you say your life is fulfilled, that you've found meaning and happiness?

Qc: No, but I'm saying we could find it, if only we could get out of this Canadian thing.

Do: Really! Do you want us to tackle that?

Qc: [*Laughing ruefully.*] Why not? At this point I have little to lose!

Do: You have been taught that fulfillment and meaning in life can be found in prosperity and self-determination.

202

Qc: Well, yes, I was taught just as you say. Mother France and the Church valued the very things you mentioned; so did the English for that matter. Everyone is preoccupied with getting their share. They walked hand in hand toward this vision. No wonder why I am wrapped up in business and the economy and property and as many games and toys as I can get. It's what they all are doing; let me get mine.

Do: Well, *mon ami*, we harvest what we have sown from the very beginning of this country.

Qc: What does that mean?

Do: Do you want to review what *Québécois* are now reaping from investing in materialism and their plethora of pleasures? Are you with me to have a look? On the Internet, I found a quick review of the problems we are dealing with here.

Qc: Oh well, let's see it then.

Do: In most of the things I'm mentioning here, we have the highest rate of the entire Canadian blended home!

Single women are abandoned in miserable conditions with their babies; poverty among single mothers is not only high but rising.

Lowest rate of birth in all provinces—tell me, is the quest for self-fulfillment preferable to family values, to investing in children?

On the news we hear weekly about sexual crimes: children and women being sexually abused.

Divorce is at about 60 percent; may I suggest that we have never learned to resolve our conflicts since we have been in North America? On the contrary, we have learned to walk away when relationships don't work; our history is a good illustration of this. Relationship for many of us triggers memories of hurt, pain, wounds; consequently we *Québécois* fear relationships: in fact we don't know how to relate. We have the lowest commitment in marriage; media and artists ridicule marriage; divorces increase the level of debt and poverty and single parent stress among *Québécois*. Gérard Gosselin, ex-deputy of *le Parti Québécois*, once said in a conference that today's family's survival is threatened in its foundation by the bombardment of modern negative influences.[237] What can I say about the tragedy of so many abortions? We pay for abortions as contraception.

Those couples who look to adopt children are now paying up to $20,000 to adopt a baby from outside the country.[238] What can we say about older and handicapped Canadian children who are eagerly and courageously awaiting an adopted home? Every unborn baby done away with is a child stolen from *Québécois* couples who desperately long to adopt a child and build a caring family and is a child losing his future before he knows he has one. In these times, can't we see that a child is a precious contribution to Quebec society, that a child's future is precious in and of itself?

Family violence: every other week, a man abuses or kills his spouse and children out of frustration and outright anger; family violence represents 25 percent of police response to crimes against persons.

The rising violence in our schools: gang fighting, stealing, drugs. In 2007, two schoolyard fights involving students resulted in murder; why should our teenagers be exposed to murder or the fear of it in order to get an education?

Highest rate of dropout: a majority of our boys have difficulty completing high school.

Alcoholism and organized crime involving drugs and gangsters: Montreal is a strategic platform in drug trafficking in North America. *Le Journal de Montréal* headline news was: "*Le Québec bon premier,*" referring to Quebec being the biggest producer of marijuana in the country. In 2006, police dealt with 3,185 cases of production in *notre belle province*, compared to British Columbia, the closest with 1,879 cases.[239]

Week after week, we hear on the news that *Québécois* are hit or killed by drunk drivers; a good portion of drunk drivers relapse; also, road rage is on the rise.

Highest rate of suicide among young adults; they are the teenagers who explored the freedom and so-called happiness promised by the preachers of secularism. *Québécois* and Native young adults have the highest rate of suicide in the world; life is meaningless—so let me out of it, and thanks for nothing! Quebec, suicide is people crying out loud, "I want to be affirmed! I am looking for meaning in life. I long to love and to be loved. I am desperate because I haven't found anything worthwhile living for! I can't find my nest..."

Rise of ethnic problems: Quebec government asks "new adopted children" (immigrants) to get integrated in Quebec culture. How can new immigrants help shape the contemporary Quebec society and have their share? *La Commission des Accomodements Raisonables* reminded us that Quebec is now a blended home and that we are getting into an era of compromises. This commission explored the growing issue of pluralistic culture and religion. However, how are *Québécois* going to handle that, since with our heritage of unresolved broken relationships we never learned to reconcile, and the whole idea of relationships keeps us worried and nervous? The commission never told us how.

We sow today, we reap tomorrow....[240]

*[Donald has been paddling briskly but stops as he finishes the list. In the canoe both can feel and enjoy a sudden fresh breeze and a few quiet moments. Donald looks back at Quebec; he sees tears in his eyes. Donald noticed Quebec wiping his eyes as discretely as possible.]*

Qc: All that bad news certainly adds to my sense of being crushed and frustrated...our troubles have just multiplied ever since we first came to North America.

Do: Does this anger, resentment, bitterness and pain you are feeling seem familiar? I have been there too—and it's not a good feeling, is it? When I realized my personal game plan to "make life work out for me *if...*" (on my terms) did not work, I started a long and painful three-year journey. But the good news is that it led me to a new window.

Qc: Did you find a window with any hope at all?

Do: Let me say it this way: your problem with the Canadian blended home is not a problem of political, economic, territorial, financial or material things. It is a spiritual problem; it is about what we value in life.

Qc: Hmm! *[Quebec's posture indicates a heavy load is on his mind.]*

Do: You see this beautiful tree on the left?

Qc: Yes.

Do: A few springtimes ago we walked by it; this tree was in bad shape—ice storm, you know. A neighbour said we could make firewood with it. Look at it now; isn't it beautiful, healthy? What we couldn't see then, but hoped, was that life still was in the tree. And when we saw buds a few weeks later, I decided to shape and prune it instead of cutting it down. Actually, this is what happened to me. After my three years in the wilderness, I was like a broken-down tree. Then, immediately following my reconciliation with God, my life was transformed and, yes, pruned and shaped too; I felt like a tree in the springtime with sweet water flowing freely, water for life and growth and blossom and fruit. I will never forget that day. It can be the same for you. Your life can be transformed.

[*Donald realizes it would be good to put the conversation on pause and let Quebec process all this.*] Oh, sorry, I'm running on. What about a canoe sprint to spend burn up some energy?

Qc: Let's go for it!

[*For another hour, they paddle—fast at times—alternately chit-chatting and silently drinking in the lakescape.*]

❖ ──────────────

236    Read 1 Corinthians 15 about hope for life.

237    Gérard Gosselin, "Le Québec, une société menacée dans ses fondements." Article written following an address given to the members and guests of the *Population et Avenir* [Population and Future] group on April 28, 1999, in Paris.

238    Ibid.

239    *Journal de Montréal*, November 28, 2007, p. 2, Unknown author.

240    Galatians 6.

# CHAPTER 13

# OPENING A NEW WINDOW...

## MIGHT THERE BE HOPE?

❧

*[When Donald and Quebec return from canoeing, they decide to cool off in the water. Lorraine joins them as they are drying themselves on the dock.]*

Lo: Hi, guys. How was the lake?

Qc: It's amazing, but I admit I am not in shape.

Do: Me too. I realize all this writing on my desktop does little for my muscles.

Qc: This lake water, it's so refreshing, so soft.

Do: The last hour was kind of challenging, wasn't it!

Lo: Donald, would you flip tonight's burgers on the grill?

Do: Yes, my dear. That's my specialty here at the lake. *[Hugs her.]*

*[Later, during supper.]*

Do: I was hungry!

Qc: Your salad is delicious, Lorraine.

Lo: Thank you; don't be shy, take some more. Salads don't store well, you know.

Qc: Your husband seems to be good enough with the grill, too.

Lo: Well, I'm not complaining. I wouldn't want to lose him, though there was a time when it seemed I might. I believe God gave me back my husband.

*[Quebec does not know what to say after Lorraine's comment. So Donald steps in.]*

Do: She means there was a time I was not there at all for her. I was too busy working at my job and personal interests. Our family life was going nowhere. Do you know what a workaholic is? My life has changed a lot.

Lo: And [*pointing a finger toward the sky*], he transformed our marriage and family!

Qc: When I hear you talk about God, it's as if he were someone real, living right next to you.

Lo: This is really what we experienced since we have been reconciled with God. Did Donald ever talk to you about his experience?

Qc: I heard him mention it few times. It's somewhat intriguing.

Lo: Would you like to hear how this happened?

Qc: Sure! I'm curious to find out more.

Lo: Take it away, Donald.

Do: During my teen years, I loved playing baseball, football and hockey. At eighteen, I began to volunteer as a sports coach, an activity that went on for fifteen years. It was while I was coaching Lorraine's brother on a hockey team that our paths crossed quite often, and Lorraine and I continued to see each other. "Your paths seem to cross continually," Lorraine's mother noticed. That relationship developed into marriage.

My obsession to outdistance everyone, whether fighting English kids on the streets of Montreal or winning at every kind of sport as an adult, was carried over into my business life. I was looking for affirmation, for success as a committed teacher, coach and sports volunteer. Now I was determined to prove I could "do it" and become a successful *homme d'affaires* in my field—which was a sports business. I won't fail this time; *I will make life work,* and I'll do it my way. As sales increased, so did the hours of work I had to put in, until I found myself on the job ninety hours a week. That went on for years and years, until I was thirty-six. Driven to find fulfillment, I had to prove myself, even at the expense of neglecting Lorraine and our children. I had to keep climbing, seeking recognition in the public world.

As for the Roman Catholic Church, I had abandoned that years ago. I remember the very spot (the intersection of Hochelaga and Hector, in Montreal) where my decision was made to ditch the Church and all its regulations. By the time I was seventeen, I felt the emptiness of my life. My religion brought me no fulfillment; I longed for something more. On my way to mass one Sunday morning, I stopped and made the decision to renounce it all. I wanted life to have some meaning but was sure I could find it in playing and coaching sports. Later, I sought yet another obsession—business success. One after another—sports, career, marriage, children, business—I pursued each project or dream, looking for public recognition. I can truly admit it now; I tried to make life work for me while leaving God out and behind me, intentionally.

For many years I augmented my business by volunteer work in sports. In 1983, my friends were organizing a big party to celebrate my fifteen years as a sports volunteer, player and coach. Several hundred were invited—my best friends from childhood and high school; key teachers of my youth; many people from the sports organization in town; Jean Corbeil, mayor of Ville d'Anjou; and to my great honour, Pierre Marc Johnson.[241] It was a gala occasion my friends had put together, with Lorraine's complicity and organizational skills! They wanted to celebrate my success and honour me as a model to others for my faithful sports involvement. Surely I had reached the top! And, so what?

That evening, my best friend, Pierre F., came to me to congratulate me. "What a party this has been, and what an honour everyone has given to you, *mon ami!*" he said. "But something puzzles me, Donald. I have never seen you look as sad as you do tonight. Tell me, what's going on?"

I had only one answer to give him. "People are so kind to me, Pierre, and I really appreciate it. It has been a great honour. but my mind keeps asking, 'Is this all there is to life?'" Was my passion to establish my personal identity and gain public recognition in life the cause of my not-so-hidden pain? If this is all life is about, it's not worth living!

I told him, "In the midst of all this public recognition, which is something I had longed for and dreamed about for years, I feel something is missing, my life is empty. At thirty-three years of age, seated on top of this pedestal, at least for this one night, it seems to wrap up the worst chapter of my life. I'm in the middle of nowhere, and I am not prepared for any 'preferred future.'"

Page 28 / FLAMBEAU DE L'EST — Mardi, le 4 octobre 1983

C'est en vraie famille que Lorraine et Donald, en compagnie de leurs enfants Martin et Claudiane, ont souri à l'oeil magique de la caméra.

Posant fièrement devant le gâteau soulignant leur 10e anniversaire de mariage; l'heureux couple, au centre, entouré de leurs parents respectifs, soit M. et Mme Marcel et Marthe Bliodeau, sans oublier M. et Mme Aurèle et Yvonne Gingras. (Photos: Gracieuseté Jean-Louis Lebrun).

Une fois de plus, Denis Perras s'est distingué comme maître de cérémonie.

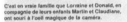

# Plein feu...

Pierre Frigon, un directeur d'école qui sait maîtriser le verbe.

Jacques Moisan, beau-frère de Donald, a effectué la première "cuisson".

M. Jean Corbeil, maire de Ville d'Anjou, nous en a rappelé de bien bonnes au sujet de Donald.

## ... sur le "bien cuit" de Donald Gingras

Un autre "cuiseur" et non le moindre, Guy Massicotte, directeur de l'information de votre Hebdo Flambeau, connaît fort bien Donald.

Bernard Roy, président sortant de l'Association du baseball mineur d'Anjou, a surpris par la rapidité de ses commentaires.

Donald et son épouse Lorraine garderont un précieux souvenir de la soirée du 24 septembre 1983. En plus de rendre hommage aux 15 ans de bénévolat du "jubilé", on a dignement souligné le 10e anniversaire de mariage du couple.

C'est avec humour que Aimé Constantin, directeur-général de la Fédération Québécoise de Football, nous a révélé quelques humbles exploits de "Ti Noir".

ABOUT THE ROAST PARTY OF DONALD GINGRAS

This was a significant moment in my life, it got my attention. To experience recognition and emptiness at the same time was troubling me. I had heard somewhere that God uses major crossroads of people's lives to connect with to them. He did so for me that evening.

Qc: I didn't know God wants to connect just as people do, or that he speaks to us.

Do: Well, he had my attention that night. For three years, life was miserably empty. Outwardly, people saw me as a model of success, seeking me out—and friends were coming to us for marriage counselling and asked what our secret was as a couple raising such nice children...yadda yadda... but trust me, deep down inside we had nothing to offer. Can one be full of emptiness? I think I was. We knew we were failing as a couple and as parents. My wife and children were unsatisfied and unimpressed with my "accomplishments"; Lorraine just wanted her husband back, while my children were longing for the dad they hardly knew well enough to miss. My ninety hours of work each week were driving me crazy, with no fulfillment of any sort. Since I had failed to make a career in hockey and baseball as an athlete, I gave up trying to have fun. Was I failing again?

During those three years, life was as satisfying as crawling in hot, arid desert sand. After our marriage, I went to mass more to please my wife, but eventually I stopped that. I was sick of playing religion. Lorraine used to get after me for not being faithful to the promise we made at the baptism—I stopped going to weekly mass.

Lo: "You are not a good example for our children," I kept repeating to make sure he understood.

Do: Tell Quebec what you did.

Lo: Go ahead, Donald; you tell him.

Do: During the time we were seeking for meaning in life, one day Lorraine, pointing her finger into my face, said, "What kind of spiritual heritage are you going to leave to your children?" Then she turned and ran off in frustration.

I was left alone with my conscience. My soul was hurting badly as I thought about her words. "What spiritual heritage *am* I going to leave to

211

my children?" I asked myself. I had no answer. Then I thought, maybe it will be only the image of a successful sports coach, a busy businessman, a workaholic father, a well-known athlete? Even though my friends saw me as a model, I knew that popularity, glory and applause were vain achievements; in fact, they troubled my soul because, despite them, I could not get satisfaction in life.

When I looked at my life, I truly acknowledged that my relationships morphed into pain, disappointment, wounds and ongoing dissatisfaction. It was painful to realize I had nothing to leave to my children but vain material security and the memory of an absentee father who had contributed no lasting happiness to their lives nor given the care they needed and who neglected their mom also! Finally, worst of all,

DONALD COACHING HOCHELAGA MIDGETS TO WIN PROVINCIAL CUP,
APRIL 1975

DONALD'S SPORTS BUSINESS 1980-87

how could I help others who came to me and my wife for counsel when I doubted my own philosophy of life? My whole life was a precarious house of cards, ready to collapse. How could I wear a mask and lie to my friends even though I genuinely desired to help those who looked up to me? Most of all, what about the future of my children? Lorraine had asked the right question!

Well, God was waiting for me at the crossroads of my empty existence...

Qc: Amazing how you went downhill! This is how I feel sometimes.

Do: And do you suspect, as I began to, that something was missing in your life, like a piece in the jigsaw puzzle?

Qc: *Mais oui*—that's exactly it.

Do: In the midst of experiencing emptiness, in 1984 I met a businessman at a bicycle sports show. Simon R. was a special guy. He had lots of experience in the bicycle business, and he offered to help me. It was unusual to see a business competitor helping a peer. In his bicycle shop, he had also a table with little Bibles available free to his customers. He used to say, "This is my secret for success." Simon R. was involved with the Gideons, you know, the organization that gives away Bibles to motels, schools, hospitals and other public establishments?

Qc: Yes, I have seen Bibles in motels.

Do: One day he told me if ever I wanted to know more about his spiritual journey he would be happy to share how he got reconciled with God and how it impacted his life. Simon started to coach me on improving my business. We became good friends.

In 1985, at Christmastime, a customer dropped into my store, needing a pair of skates. We began to talk. "What do you do for a living?" I asked him, as I did every customer. "I am a pastor," he replied. "Tell me about that," I said. I wanted to know more. Why did he seem so contented?

"We learn to live by following God." This conversation started a relationship with Claude V. I was intrigued by those two guys who were paying attention to God and the Bible in their lives. Furthermore, I was impressed by their genuine conversation and lifestyle.

That initiated a fourteen-month process that led Lorraine and me to reconciliation with God. I began to read the Bible. I was thrilled to be reading truths I had never heard before; I couldn't stop reading. Surely this must be the way to truth about life! My feelings of life's utter futility, of fear that our marriage might fall apart at any time, of bitterness toward the "anti-French" segment of Canada and my "religious" belief in nationalism and *l'état providence*—were these the causes of my secret pain? Had I been climbing the wrong ladder? How could I find healing for so many broken, painful relationships? Was any peace available?

My friend Simon R. and his wife invited us for supper. After enjoying their bountiful table, we talked about how practical following God really is. Simon explained to us how he got reconciled with God and how his life had been transformed as a result. This is the first time I had ever heard such an idea; he explained it in the simplest way. Jesus, the Son of God, died on the cross to provide reconciliation between

God and men. The Bible says: "*All this is from God, who **reconciled** us to himself through Christ and gave us the ministry of **reconciliation**: that God was **reconciling** the world to himself in Christ, not counting men's sins against them.*" He explained that sin involves walking independently from God's plan and therefore breaking our relationship with him. And also that Jesus paid the penalty for our sin with his death, and his success in doing so was evident through his resurrection from the dead. "*And he has committed to us the ministry of **reconciliation**. We are therefore Christ's ambassadors, as though God were making his appeal through us. We implore you in Christ's behalf: Be **reconciled** to God.*"[242]

Qc: This is certainly all about full reconciliation!

Do: Full reconciliation, just as you say! I wonder how any individual, organization, church or even religion can call themselves Christian if they are not genuinely committed to live and model reconciliation Jesus' way? And this includes all kinds of relationships: marriage, family, community and nation.

Qc: This is a straightforward question. It is obvious; I know a lot of people who would have to examine themselves seriously...starting with me first!

Do: God loves the world, simply and truly. And I understood that the missing piece in my life was God-shaped and it could join together the rest of the puzzle, filling that painful hole. My friend Simon explained to us that God is a personality who made us and is seeking to have a personal relationship with each one of us.

During the following week, Lorraine and I started to read the Bible each day. It seems the Bible became more vivid; it took on new meaning, as if there was life in it. Claude V. came into my sports shop; as usual, we drank coffee and talked. That Thursday afternoon, my store was really getting busy with customers buying bicycles. Lorraine and I felt compelled to ask many practical questions about the Bible and our lives. I knew somehow that very day was important, an appointment we could not miss. It seemed that God was there in the store along with all the customers; his presence seemed to command my attention—I needed to pursue the conversation he wanted to initiate. I asked my employees to take care of the customers so I could have an important meeting; I invited Claude and Lorraine to come to my basement office where we could quietly continue our conversation. God came along with us!

After a brief discussion, we were led in a simple prayer in which we asked God to be reconciled with him. I remember saying, "God, you know how my life is messy, how I feel my life is like a dog chasing his tail, going nowhere; I feel empty without you. Would you forgive me, for I have offended you for trying to make life work by myself, selfishly—outside of your plan and leaving you out? I now commit my life to you. God, use it as you wish; my life is yours."

Qc: You prayed as you might talk to a person!

Do: Yes, I did and do. God became real and present in my life. The Bible teaches that Jesus is the Son of God and the way to God. He is waiting for each one of us: *"Here I am! I stand at the door and knock. If anyone hears my voice and opens the door, I will come in and eat with him, and he with me."*[243] That day, March 20th, 1986, I opened the door of my life to Jesus. I received and accepted God's forgiveness and experienced peace with him.[244] Life has never been the same since. From that moment, God began to transform our hearts and lives for the better.

Qc: What about you, Lorraine?

Lo: I also asked for forgiveness and got reconciled with God. God had a lot to transform in my life, too, to make me a better mother and wife. From this special moment, things began to change for us. God gave me back my husband!

Qc: Now I see what you meant. You and Donald were reconciled because each of you was reconciled with God.

Do: From the undesirable husband, father and citizen I was before, God enabled me to be reconciled with my wife, my children and, later, other people I had offended. And yes, first I was reconciled with him.

Lo: Donald started to spend time with our children, with me; we improved our communication to a deeper level and in important subjects. A new adventure had started; our spirits were renewed day by day as we read God's plan for our lives—I mean the teaching in the Bible.

Qc: It is so simple. I wonder why it was never explained this way to us.

Lo: Yes. Getting reconciled with God is not complicated; he is waiting for everyone to come and be reconciled with him. God longs for a personal relationship with us.

Do: Jesus said, *"Whoever comes to me I will never drive away."*[245]

Qc: I am very impressed by your faith. With my background, God for me was more like a stately building, coming to mass, religious traditions—you know, the duties and ceremonies. What you talk about is so different....

[*Moment of silence, then Lorraine pours coffee.*]

Lo: Let me clear the table and serve dessert.

Qc: Thank you for coffee, Lorraine, but I am full; I will pass on dessert.

Do: I will also, Lorraine, but what about marshmallows and a fire? The evening is perfect for it.

[*After supper, the three enjoy a stroll around the lake.*]

❧ ————————————————

[241]    I knew Pierre-Marc Johnson well as my MP and from social involvement in Ville d'Anjou county. He was in the Department of Social Affairs from April 30, 1981, to March 5, 1984. He was elected president of the *Parti Québécois* on September 29, 1985. He was premier of Québec and president of the *Conseil exécutif* from October 3 to December 12, 1985.

[242]    2 Corinthians 5:18-20.

[243]    Revelation 3:20.

[244]    1 John 1:9.

[245]    John 6:37.

CHAPTER 14

# WINDOW OF HOPE...
# AND RECONCILIATION

⚜

*[Later, outdoors around the fire.]*

Qc: What a sunset. How often do you get a day like this? And so...wholesome, I guess. Walking, canoeing, swimming eating...good conversations. It has been a long time since I had such a...well, uplifting experience, I would say, a time to think.

Do: I enjoyed my day too, and our conversations. Were they too heavy?

Qc: Since when do I run away from heavy talk!

Lo: So, you enjoyed your rest?

Qc: This day really made me think. I like the way you live your faith. It seems real, practical. And I like the relationship you have with each other, if you don't mind me saying so.

Do: The thing I am most thankful for is that God led us to discover the message of reconciliation.

Qc: Hmm! *[Some silence.]* On the lake, you mentioned that the problem of Canada's blended family is a spiritual problem.

Do: Yes, I am convinced it is.

Qc: What does religion have to do with this? Don't you think we've had enough of religion? I have started to believe that most religions are man-made, self-serving and more and more questionable.

Do: I agree. You sound like many of my friends and relatives. A big disappointment I have is that when I want to talk about God to my friends, they avoid the subject, because they have an idea of what

219

religions have done to our country and how many religions are causing wars, terrorism and abuse in the world by selling illusions and offering false happiness to their followers. Yet many conclude that it's somehow God's fault.

Qc: But we don't need more religion, do we!

Do: I agree. Tell me, Québec, what was Adam and Eve's religion?

Qc: [*Hesitant.*] I don't really know...I never heard they had a religion; it was more a relationship with God in the garden, as far as I know.

Do: The Bible teaches that, as with Adam and Eve, God is looking for a relationship with his children; he has no interest in man-made religions. But just as pride led Adam and Eve to abandon God's plan and break the relationship, so human beings have the tendency to find fulfillment through self-oriented projects, seeking control and power as they try to make life work out independently from God. In this way we human beings organize religions to serve our egoistic goals and ambitions.

Lo: On the other hand, through a shocking and powerful demonstration of humility, Jesus came to earth first of all to reconnect people with the Creator of the universe and, I would say, to abolish man-made organized religion and to establish God's kingdom on earth.

Qc: But many Canadians do say this country was founded on Christianity.

Do: As far as we know, great and significant efforts have been made by Christian individuals, churches and organizations. But to understand the situation here, we need to take a look at our last 400 years of history and to ask what kind of Christianity has been demonstrated by religious leaders and churches and what sort of values and motivations drove their decisions and action as they built the country.

Qc: What do you think?

Do: A historical survey helps us to see that many efforts certainly contributed to bring and to spread the heritage of Judeo-Christian values we talked about earlier.

Qc: But what I heard is that the fathers of the 1867 Canadian Confederation deliberately chose their motto "from sea to sea" on the basis of the Bible (Psalm 72, verse 8): *"He will rule from sea to sea."* And, for this reason, that makes Canada a Christian country.

Do: Some of these fathers shared this belief; and yes, this is part of our Christian heritage. Although it seems that a few Christian concepts have been built into Canada during the course of four centuries of our history, it is vital to understand that we are talking about the foundation on which the country rests. Confederation came about in 1867; in other words, 333 years after Jacques Cartier planted his cross (1534). So this means French, First Nations and English people had been competing, fighting with each other for three centuries for business and land. In fact, this historical check demonstrates that Canada's real foundations were laid on a materialistic—you know, a business and possession—mindset. Every country that came to North America did so to take possession of the goods and resources here. The world economy was entering a big expansion, and they wanted to be in on the ground floor, so to speak. Most of what was called Christian then was really the late medieval Roman Catholic politico-religious system... and, with no doubt, we can affirm that these were the main foundations on which Canada was built and developed afterwards.

Lo: Let me give you an example. It's like any dysfunctional family whose members have been fighting and in conflict with each other for years and years; and, one day, as they make their union and blended home status official, they decide to display a crucifix in the living room to sincerely express their belief in God along with their new beginning. Does that make them a Christian family? Does that resolve the heritage of their unresolved conflicts? Does that bring healing to their ongoing hurts and wounds? Does that transform their lives?

Qc: Of course not! It can be sincere, but it can be a religious move too. I can relate to that. We experienced that sort of piety; and, I should add, it did not change our lives; as a result today, most of our traditional churches are empty. I know what you are talking about. In fact, after reading the report of *La Commission des Accomodements Raisonables (May 2008)*, Jean Charest, the Premier of Quebec, announced that his government will make a law to permanently display the crucifix in the National

Assembly because it represents a "cultural connotation of 350 years in history," he said. We all know it's a symbol, it won't change our lives and it won't transform Quebec, nor resolve the actual cultural and religious problems of both the *Québécois* and Canadian blended homes. It's more for "*Je me souviens..*," one more thing to remember about our past.

Lo: And, like this hurting home we just described, when Canada became an official blended family (in 1867), its foundations represented three centuries of dysfunctional relationships and competing spirits; Canada was built on this heritage. You know, Quebec, Jesus' vision for society was to deal with and bring solutions to human problems and conflicts, to establish God's justice, and bring a new set of beliefs and values and spiritual renewal that would transform lives, families, and even communities. Following Jesus' teaching and model, his disciples experienced amazing results living a Christian lifestyle. Jesus encourages us to build our spiritual home on solid ground (the rock), so when the storm comes, it really stands. But when the rain comes down, the stream rises, and the winds blow and beat against them, those who built on weak foundations (on the sand) will fall with a great crash, Jesus said.[246] Have we built on the rock or on the sand? The results speak for themselves, don't they? Today, we are still reaping the negative consequences of this heritage of hurts and wounds of broken relationships and of pattern of unresolved and ongoing conflicts. Let me add that many of the early efforts to christianize Canada, although they were sincere, could not lay in place a truly Christ-centred foundation; Christianity is relational and about heart transformation, reconciliation, compassion and love for God and with each other. Most of what we are seeing today is far away from the sort of Christianity the Bible teaches about.

Qc: Okay, agreed. Now, can you explain to me how French, Native and English conflicts and problems are of a spiritual nature?

Do: French Catholics and English Protestants were competing to control the fur trade and occupy the land. The adventurers of both nations modelled a lifestyle of worldly ambition, competitiveness, division, racism and militarism. They brought their traditional rivalry from Europe, of course. Sure, there were Roman Catholic missionary priests for the Indians; probably they did the best of all the early priests and ministers of other religious groups who came. But the clergy for the Europeans worked within the context of legitimizing the competitive fur trade and the nationalistic territorial conquest.

Qc: Are you saying that enterprise shaped the religion more than the religion shaped enterprise?

Do: That's a good way of seeing it. As a result, French and English Canadians have inherited not only this natural aversion to each other but also a negative experience and understanding of religion, including the type of Christianity they experienced. Then, living in the parish for 200 years, isolated and separated from our English neighbours and the rest of the world, we adopted our parish mindset, which had a kind of separatist element in it. No doubt Protestant English Christianity had its own issues. So these negative aspects are what French Canadians and many of the English who came here knew of Christianity and practised.

Qc: From what I hear and read from credible surveys, *Québécois* are still searching for God, but, at the same time, they are not looking for church buildings or a new organized religion.

Do: Yes, you and I are observing the same phenomenon, and I agree with you. But something really bothers me.

Qc: What is it?

Do: With this race and fight for fur trade and business and to possess the land and economy of North America, and with the distorted varieties of Christianity that came to and were demonstrated within Canada, we have been robbed from knowing the message of Reconciliation. If Jesus would come back today, would he even recognize the Christianity he established with his apostles? All too often, the organised Church failed to bring people the life-changing gospel; also, the clergy did not teach, lead and coach people to experience reconciliation with God and with each other. Later, *Québécois*, and other Canadians as well, walked away en masse from the Church, in confused frustration.

Qc: You are comparing seventeenth century European religion with the message of reconciliation that transformed your life, aren't you!

Do: Precisely. It was not politics or more money or more power, a new treaty or religion that changed me into a new husband, father and citizen.

Qc: I see. You are talking about the teachings of Jesus, aren't you?

Do: *Oui*. Jesus did not come to earth to gain political power, but he came to offer reconciliation and loving relationships with God through faith and with one another. It wasn't about religion at all, though human beings have been remarkably effective in "religionizing" it! It is through the message of reconciliation that we can find a healing perspective for our Canadian heritage of broken relationships among the French, the Native people and the English and now our new adopted immigrants. Don't you see our blended multi-ethnic country needs healing?

Qc: Yes, I truly believe so! So you believe Jesus doesn't have much to do with religion, the sort that Canadians have deserted?

Lo: We read about Jesus, and he hardly mentioned or discussed religion, and when he did, he pointed out the problems in it! His interest was in God's mission to us, to bring God's message, as I said previously.

Do: It's worth repeating it, Jesus was not in the business of developing an earthly political and material empire or building majestic buildings. He came to establish God's Kingdom on earth. Jesus' message was so powerful in transforming the lives of hurting and conflicted individuals, families, communities and nations that political and religious leaders were afraid they would lose control of people (and their kingdoms).

Qc: Is this the reason why Jesus had so much opposition from politicians and religious leaders?

Lo: That would make sense to me. Everywhere Jesus and his disciples were, lives were being transformed; they had so much influence. Look how they turn the world upside down. Two thousand years later, we are still reaping the benefits from the life-changing faith and values they powerfully preached, taught, modeled and propagated.

Qc: We cannot deny these benefits. I really agree with you. Thank God for this!

Do: Jesus always confronted social justice and unfair political issues. He also denounced the Pharisees, the prevailing politico-religious group around him; they misled the people by ruling over them and imposing a religion of laws and traditions they could not fulfill themselves.

Qc: Laws and traditions are not good?

Do: Not that any one of those was evil, but the system trapped them because the Pharisees refused to admit that it is impossible to fulfill the law to perfectly please God. They knew the laws God had given to their forefathers, but they fabricated a huge body of rituals and traditions to be tantamount to the instructions of God, with the result that they kept people in bondage to the law.

Qc: Who were those men who made religious laws and traditions?

Lo: They were the zealous religious people who really loved the law, but they had no loving, reconciled relationship with God. Jesus once said to them, *"And why do you break the command of God for the sake of your tradition?*[247] *You have let go of the commands of God and are holding on to the traditions of men."*[248] The problem with the Pharisees is that they made a religion that locked God in their temple with man-made rituals and traditions. Jesus came to make God live where he should be: in the hearts of people. Indeed, the Bible says we are the temple of God and the temple of the Holy Spirit,[249] it's obvious that God wants a personal relationship with us. Jesus said, *"Love the Lord your God with all your heart and with all your soul and with all your strength and with all your mind; and, 'Love your neighbor as yourself.'"*[250] Christianity has to do with transformation of the heart in the context of an intimate relationship with God; this is where it starts.

Qc: It's a straightforward approach to life. Almost too simple!

Do: Somehow, every new survey indicates that the *Québécois* are still searching for God. As I listen to them, I believe they are looking for an unknown God...who can provide lasting love, care, justice and peace. Human beings are born for love and to be loved; it's at the core of our being. We long for love.

Qc: It really makes sense. *Yes*, people walk for peace because of wars, conflict, injustice....

Do: We have to be careful with people who call for peace! Peace! Peace!

Qc: Why is that?

Do: I know *Québécois* who have walked in the streets of Montreal for peace, a demonstration against war, terrorism, abuse; these are legitimate causes to support. I also know a few who walked for peace with the flag of Quebec in their hands, calling for peace but ironically giving the message they want to separate at any cost, even though they know they could hurt their neighbours. How can they walk for peace?

I know *Québécois* who walked for peace, but they run well when hurting their spouse, breaking their marital union...how can they walk for peace?

I know *Québécois* who walked for peace, but they run as they abandon and hurt their children causing them lifelong wounds...how can they walk for peace? I could go on with the list. These are a kind of people who look "cool" on surface, walking for peace as they sing Raymond Lévesque's song "*Quand les hommes vivront d'amour; ce sera la paix sur la terre*" (when men will live by love, there will be peace on earth), but what are their real motives for walking? On one hand they say "stop the war and terrorism" because they don't want it in their backyard; on the other hand, ironically, they take actions that hurt people by their "me-myself-and-I" self-serving lifestyle.

Qc: Don't get me wrong here, I don't want to sound like I'm regurgitating! It reminds me of some people who had a hand in the shameful Sponsorship scandal, and who walked in the streets of Montreal before the 1995 referendum shouting, "I love you Quebec!" Isn't this what you are talking about?

Do: Point taken! No need to elaborate on this here [*all laughing together*].

Qc: So, you are not against walking for peace?

Do: No, as I said, I believe there are legitimate causes; for example just think how meaningful and fruitful were Martin Luther King's walks in the streets across the U.S. to claim social justice between black and white people. Listen to this wise principle, "*Dear children, let us not love with words or tongue but with actions and in truth. This is how we know we*

226

*are from the truth,*"[251] I understand that our life needs to match our words if we want to make a difference in our world.

Qc: What should people do?

Do: If you really and wholeheartedly want to fight war and terrorism, you ought to start in your own life, as a couple, family, neighbourhood, and community; this is where you can make a difference by engaging responsibly into genuine relationships. The power of Jesus' message is that it transforms people where the personal rubber hits the road. You can be a spectator or be part of those who work at making a difference. Anybody can take part in a walk for peace in the street...it's easy. But not everybody is willing to engage in Jesus' challenging path of reconciliation. What is your choice?

Qc: All over the planet now, people are looking for peace. The safest places, like Canada was before, are now vulnerable.

Lo: There was a time in my life when I cried out to God for peace in my marriage, my family and in my own heart!

Do: People need God, though many don't realize what he can do for them. Until we get reconciled with God—obviously, the God of reconciliation—and experience it with each other, I don't see how we can get lasting peace. We are built for more than wars, terrorism, violence or abuse. In our day, people feed the illusion that we live in a more civilized world, that we are more evolved.

Lo: Are we living in a better world, a more mature world and a world where we are more responsible in our human relationships? Watch the news, read the newspapers...it is about evolution, in which the strongest will survive.

Qc: Evolution like this I don't want!

Do: Culture is always changing, though faithfully following the drumbeats by which a society marches on.

Qc: I agree.

Do: On the other hand, there is another drumbeat to which we can march. When I was reconciled with God, my friend Simon explained to me how the Bible teaches that God's timeless instructions provide wisdom and blessings to those who practice them. He explained to me that Jesus said in the Bible, "*I am the way, the truth and the life.*" Take him at his word; he will never lie to you, Simon said.

Qc: What do you think about this statement?

Lo: For over twenty years, Jesus has never disappointed us. Where we found out some cultures might lead to confusion and division among men, we discovered how God's plan is reconciling with love and then providing wisdom and peace.

Do: World history proves to us that generally man-made peace doesn't last and does not heal broken relationships and wounds. I understand today that peace is a fruit, the result of a genuine reconciliation, first with God and second with each other; the gospel is about peace.[252]

Qc: I never heard about the gospel of peace and reconciliation! Our story in North America is one of a constant battle for survival against the English and...anyway, you all know about this!

Do: Jesus said, "*Peace I leave with you; my peace I give you. I do not give to you as the world gives. Do not let your hearts be troubled and do not be afraid.*"[253] And Jesus came to reconcile human beings to God and to each other; this is where peace lives. "*This is how we know what love is: Jesus Christ laid down his life for us. And we ought to lay down our lives for our brothers.*"[254]

Qc: This is challenging. We are not used to hearing such teaching.

Do: Yes, a real challenge. There is always a price to pay for reconciliation. The question remains: do you want to make a difference?

Lo: Quebec, can I ask you a personal question?

[*Quebec, feeling well accepted by his hosts and safe, opens up freely as they sit by the fire.*]

Qc: Sure! Go ahead.

Lo: I once asked this question to my husband, "What kind of spiritual heritage are you going to leave to your children, to future generations?"

Qc: Well, it is an important question...[*Pause.*]

[*The question brings painful memories; Quebec reviews his life. "What am I going to leave my children? The heritage of Mother France? Of the Church? Of l'état providence? Of our struggles with the English? Of the preachers of secular postmodern culture? Of the nationalists? Of the Canadian*

228

*Charter of Rights and Freedoms? My heritage of pain and wounds caused by multiplication of unresolved and ongoing broken relationships? Our French language as a cultural icon? Environmental pollution? My search for business achievement? Financial debt? What do I have that is worthwhile to leave?"*
*He cannot yet answer.]*

Qc: Talking about reconciliation, what about all those who hurt me? Should they not admit their fault and apologize for all they did to us?

Do: Fair question. What about those who invaded, used, abused and hurt the Native people? What about those who rejected, persecuted and murdered the Huguenots? What about the practice of slavery with black people in New France?

Qc: Umm, that would be us, wouldn't it. Well, we learned to keep our distance from the people who hurt us. We never learned reconciliation, especially not to initiate it; we have usually focused on ourselves. After all, we were the *victim* in all this. As for the Natives and Huguenots...well, I suppose they're inconvenient truths, aren't they. I will never be able...It is unthinkable to initiate reconciliation!

Lo: Can I share with you how we witnessed the power of reconciliation while travelling and speaking across Canada?

Qc: How was that?

Lo: During our tour, each time Donald shared the story of Quebec the grown-up orphan, the outcome was eye-opening. The thought patterns of many people concerning the broken relationships among French, Native and English people were challenged or even transformed, right there in front of us as Donald spoke and people listened intently.

Do: I wish you could have been there. At the end of each message, Lorraine joined me, held my hand, and she said to the audience, "We learned from living three years in Western Canada how many of you have been hurt through relationships and battles with Quebec. We cannot deny it—it's your reality; we could see it while observing from your window. For this reason, we ask for your forgiveness for the hurts and pain we caused you."

Qc: Something I don't understand. You spoke on the story of the grown-up orphan, the hurts and wounds he had to suffer, and as a victim, you ask for forgiveness.

Do: I agree it does not really make sense. It is not as a victim that I ask for forgiveness but as one sorry for my wrongdoings; it works. It started with this man in Saskatchewan in 1988 when we experienced reconciliation after I asked him to forgive us, and it has always been the same since. Even though one is a victim, reconciliation has to be initiated in good faith by admitting one's wrongdoings and by readiness to forgive others; this must be done without putting any expectation on the other party. Although we have no control over people, on our part, we can initiate reconciliation. Everywhere we went, with no exception, we witnessed the power of reconciliation: people owning up to their personal wrongdoings and judgmental spirit toward the *Québécois*, people lining up after conferences to share how much they see themselves in the message, asking us to forgive them, testimonies of others sharing that this message opened for them a new understanding of Quebec and Canada relationships.

Lo: No wonder why one suggestion came over and over: "Get this story written; it helps so much to look at our history through this new window. It makes a difference to understand how we failed in our relationships while being too preoccupied by politics, business and organized religion. Canadians ought to see through this window."

[*Solemn silence.*]

So tell me, Quebec, did keeping your distance resolve any conflicts among the French, the Native people and the English? People like to believe separation or elapsed time resolves conflict and heals broken relationships. That's not so. Look at the ethnic conflicts in Europe, the Middle East mess and African tribal warfare. Is that an acceptable outcome? Wounds need to be healed at their roots.

Qc: [*Gazes into the fire.*] It's obvious...when I explore deep inside, I am not happy...You heard enough today of my frustrations and broken relationships, haven't you?

Lo: Did you hear the recent public apology of our Roman Catholic bishop, Mgr Ouellet, who asked forgiveness for major mistakes made by the Roman Catholic Church? Discrimination toward women, homosexuals and First Nation people, children molested by priests, power abuse, anti-Semitism, racism, mothers forced to procreate: *"L'église fait son mea-culpa."*[255]

Qc: That was quite a step, wasn't it? It made headlines! but, there was criticism as well. Some thought he was feigning repentance. What do you think?

Do: Actually, I believe this is one step in the right direction. It's not for us to judge. Mgr Ouellet is accountable for his own heart motives and actions. We really need to welcome this courageous initiative.

Lo: As far as we know, this is the first time in 400 years of Quebec's history that a Roman Catholic leader in high authority has acknowledged and asked forgiveness for some wrongdoings of the Church. Amazing—this is history!

Do: Reconciliation is not a "quick fix"; it's a process. Every genuine effort must be encouraged. Remember, reconciliation has the power to transform the lives of people; to forgive will lead to lasting healing, peace and joy.

Qc: I can accept this. I guess we will see eventually what comes out of this.

Do: *Oui!* What really matters is not to find who is guilty, whose fault it was. Nor is it a way to find a scapegoat for our problems. You know, Quebec, I did not write my book to rewrite history or to make accusations and promote an unforgiving spirit, hatred, anger or resentment toward France, the Roman Catholic Church, the English, or any other group of people for injuries they inflicted on the French Canadians and *Québécois*. Fairness required we not forget those we injured too...so we might examine the motives of our wounded hearts and see how we respond to our wounds. Are we hurting people back as a result? My book is about looking through your history and the Canadian blended home from another window...the window of reconciliation!

Lo: If you'll allow me....

Qc: Yes, go ahead, Lorraine.

Lo: In the process of reconciliation, as I said previously, each accepts his responsibility, admits his wrongdoings, forgives the others and commit to restoring relationships. In this situation at least, there is no such thing as one being 100 percent guilty, 100 percent the victim, being a winner or a loser. Indeed, people who experience genuine reconciliation are all winners, and their relationships grow healthy. And no matter what the other party does, our responsibility is to be honest about our own actions and to offer forgiveness to others. This is the reconciliation that Jesus modelled, the path in which Jesus sets people free.

Qc: Wow! Need a capital "R" for *reconciliation*, don't we! What a challenge!

Do: Reconciliation is the missing ingredient in the Canadian blended home. It has a lot of potential to help us move to a renewed national vision. Reconciliation is our Canadian challenge.

Qc: But don't you think that to resolve conflict we ought to find the truth somehow?

Do: Yes. Truth is a necessary prelude to reconciliation. You've heard of the Truth and Reconciliation Commission that is dealing with the Natives and the residential schools, *non?* Reconciliation requires that wrongdoing be acknowledged and forgiveness be given. It is the starting

232

point. We do not control other people's lives, but we can control ours. It starts with you and me as we implement the instruction of God's Word.

Qc: Hmm! It sounds unusual, challenging!

Do: It's a process. but don't worry about all that has to be done; just start the process.

Qc: Where to start, Donald?

Do: Jesus said, *"If you hold to my teaching, you are really my disciples. Then you will know the truth, and the truth will set you free."*[256] The truth Jesus was talking about is crucial; it's the truth that can make the difference.

Qc: What *did* matter to him?

Do: What mattered for Jesus was that people express their suffering, wounds and needs and also admit honestly their own faults and ask God forgiveness for their wrongdoings toward God (for leaving him behind, walking in life independently) and toward others. It all comes back to reconciliation. What do you think?

Qc: No, please go on!

Do: There are two aspects of truth we have to look at. One is the truth that led people to experience pain, trouble, suffering and broken relationships. That is painful truth, what human beings do to themselves and each other when they are acting selfishly. This side of the truth has to be acknowledged, confessed...which is not good news, although it is a necessity to figure out what's wrong.

Lo: Another truth is the good news side Jesus was talking about. He talked about a truth that sets people free, the message of reconciliation. It asked us to renounce our rights, vengeance and destructive actions, to lay down pride and act with humility, to listen and care compassionately for each other. The result of love, compassion and acceptance is healed relationships. Getting free opens up the door to all kinds of good things: we are created for a higher purpose and meaning in life, and they are achievable once we have agreed with God and accepted his gracious help. *"For everything in the world—the cravings of sinful man, the lust of his eyes and the boasting of what he has and does—comes not from* [God] *the Father but from the world. The world and its desires pass away, but the man who does the will of God lives forever."*[257]

Qc: I never heard about truth this way.

Do: Well, I am speaking of truth but also grace. Grace is goodness that flows to us from God and out of his infinite love; in the situation we are discussing, it is the divinely given capacity for people to walk through life while following the pathway of reconciling love. How many times have we heard *"Vive le Québec libre!"* as Quebec longed to be free? Did a slogan like that help to solve the Canadian blended family problems? Slogans and songs are okay, but they don't transform lives or set people free or bring healing to the wounds.

Lo: Don't you think God has a higher calling for the *Québécois*, the English majority and our First Nations-Inuit-Metis people and newly adopted Canadians? The truth is, we are built for more than the achievements, possessions and wealth of this world. These can't bring lasting peace in life anyway.

Qc: But we live in this world, don't we?

Do: Of course; we are in the world, and worldly matters have their place, but Jesus was very clear about needing to go beyond these things. In fact, *"Give to Caesar what is Caesar's, and to God what is God's,"* Jesus said on this issue.[258] We have to learn to walk God's way while living as well as possible in this world! Jesus asked this deeply penetrating question, *"What good will it be for a man if he gains the whole world, yet forfeits his soul?"*[259]

Qc: Donald, I guess you've gone far away from being a separatist? A sovereignist? And what do you say about *Québec libre*?

Do: Well, actually I believe in Quebec removed as far as possible from slavery to the illusions, possessions, desires and power of this world. So...yes! I am a separatist, believing we should separate ourselves from wrongdoing, whether abuse, conflicts and wars or just our petty actions and attempts to make life work out by our self-centred choices independent of God's plan. And...*surprise*, Quebec, I am a sovereignist, too. I believe in the sovereignty of God and in Jesus' gospel of reconciliation to be over Quebec and the Rest of Canada. And I would shout *Vive le Québec libre* as well—because I believe in a *Québec libre*, free from living with the illusion that life will work out if we selfishly strive to possess the world—especially at the expense of others and while refusing the relationship God is offering us.

*[They laugh at the irony of Donald's re-interpretation and then reflect silently as they toast a new round of marshmallows.]*

Lo: Quebec, what kind of spiritual heritage are you going to leave to your children?

*[Quebec looks up, brushing the corner of his eye.]*

Qc: I hope for a good one, but...many things in my life speak for themselves. All the relationships I have engaged in since I came to America are broken, and I still feel the rejection. I'm just like you said, Donald. I lost my parents and family in the pursuit of this fur-trade adventure. I cannot trust other human beings—life has proven that. I feel that nobody loves me or has really been faithful to care for me or affirm me. Why should they? I am grown up, but they don't know that inside I am hurting like an orphan and there is still a little boy in me looking for his family. I feel I am alone...*[Quebec's eyes have brimmed up.]*

Do: I appreciate your honesty. And, it's okay to admit that what we invested in and aimed toward in life has failed to bring lasting satisfaction or real happiness, and it's even valuable to recognize a significant failure in life.

*[Quebec allows his emotions their freedom.]*

Lo: You said nobody cares for you, loves you, affirms you. But I strongly believe that God cares for you, your family, your community...he understands your feelings of rejection because he has been rejected himself. But, most important, he is waiting to comfort you. Come to him and be reconciled with him first. Reconciling with God is like a husband and wife reconciling after a painful separation, where they were walking away from each other, going in opposite directions. To be reconciled, you need to acknowledge your wrongdoing and forgive as Jesus did others. *"Forgive us our debts, as we also have forgiven our debtors."*[260] This is the starting point.

Qc: It sounds as if it might work. *[With sadness.]* I guess I left him out of my life and walked the other way.

Lo: How can we say we love God and then leave him out of our lives? Can we only call for him when we are stuck in the mud, when things go wrong? God wants more than to play the role of Santa Claus in your life. People call on God for healing. How many people after they have been healed, walk away from God again?[261] God longs for an intimate relationship with you.

Do: God is a caring Father for his children. We need to allow him this role. When we do, he brings us into his family, a family that reflects God's love, care and values to live by. By the way, God's family is a blended family, filled with adopted children who have been reconciled with him.[262] The Canadian blended family is dysfunctional, messy, hopeless; but the good news is that God has his way of redeeming and healing any broken homes that open up to him, and he wants to transform lives, marriages, families, communities and nations. He wants to show the power of his truth to transform lives and make them all they can become.

Lo: He is just waiting for us to open ourselves up to him. "*In love he predestined us to be adopted as his sons through Jesus Christ.*"[263] "*For you did not received a spirit that makes you a slave again to fear, but you received the Spirit of sonship. And by him we cry, 'Abba, Father.' The Spirit himself testifies with our spirit that we are God's children.*"[264]

Qc: An amazing plan—believable, actually! I really admire you guys for your love of the teachings of the Bible; it speaks to me. I am sincerely touched by the wisdom, peace and boldness that emerge from you.

Do: Have you read the popular slogan: "When everything else fails, read the instructions?"

Qc: Interesting! I see where you are going. You are talking about the instructions of the Bible, aren't you?

Lo: In the last twenty years, we have learned how good and vital it is to rely on God's wisdom for everyday living. I tell you, it is worth living for a loving God who is so committed to reconciliation. It is the greatest discovery we ever made; it is worth investing in God's instructions and experiencing them in our lives.

Qc: I see your point.

[*Quebec is reviewing in his mind a recent survey of* Sondage Léger-Le Journal, "Les *Québécois* en panne de valeurs: Perdus sans religion" *(The Québécois in crisis of values: Lost without religion). The survey was reminding Quebec that while a majority of Québécois believe in God (78 percent) and in Jesus (83 percent), some also think that they have lost their cultural identity, that religion was important and the society has lost some a sense of moral values.*265]

[*Quebec is thinking it over.* "What good will it be for a man if he gains the whole world, yet forfeits his soul?266 *What kind of spiritual heritage am I going to leave to my children?" "When everything else fails, read the instructions...." There is sadness on Quebec's face. Lorraine quietly wonders, as Donald had earlier, "Is his sadness arising from a feeling of guilt? Or, is it sadness that leads to repentance, to humility, to reconciliation with God?"*267

*Meanwhile, a familiar old song runs through Donald's mind.*

*"Amazing grace, how sweet the sound..." At the same time, a promise from the Bible—* "The LORD is near to all who call on him, to all who call on him in truth...He hears their cry..."268 *intermingles with the song...prompting Donald to one last, gentle, vital question.*]

237

Do: What would stop you from wanting to be reconciled with God? Quebec, God is waiting for you.

[*The embers glow red, and each person gazes reflectively into their brightness and embraces the warmth.*]

❧ ——————————————————————

246  Matthew 7:24-27

247  Matthew 15:2-3.

248  Mark 7:8.

249  1 Corinthians 3:16; 6:19.

250  Luke 10:27.

251  1John 3:18.

252  Ephesians 6:15.

253  John 14:27.

254  1 John 3:16.

255  "L'Église fait son mea-culpa," *Journal de Montréal*; mercredi, 21 Novembre, 2007. Front page and 2, 3, 30.

256  John 8:31-32.

257  1 John 2:16-17.

258  Matthew 22:21.

259  Matthew 16:26.

260  Matthew 6:12.

261  In the parable of the ten healed of leprosy, Jesus healed ten but only one came back to thank him, while the nine others went on their way. Luke 17:17-19.

262  John 1:12.

263  Ephesians 1:5.

264  Romans 8:15.

265  *Journal de Montréal*, March 17, 2008, front page; full survey, *Sondage Léger-Le Journal*, pp. 2-5.

266    Matthew 16:26.

267    2 Corinthians 7:10 talks about two kinds of sorrow: the repentant sorrow that produces a change of attitude and the unrepentant one that produces death. In other words, real repentance leads to change, to a genuine transformation of the heart.

268    Psalm 145:18.

# The First Nations, Inuit and Métis and Reconciliation

If the Québécois have been an orphan foster child in the blended Canadian family, and if reconciliation is crucial for the recovery of the blended family, then the question arises, "What does this make the First Nations, Inuit and Métis people who live in Canada?" Certainly they are children in the blended Canadian family. Perhaps they could be viewed as foster children with only Earth for their natural mother, but through her, they have a prior claim on the orphanage facility itself—one that none of the other Europe-based children have. If this comparison is true, the new parent (Mother England) can be imagined moving into the orphanage to displace the (Ab)original parent. The new parent begins to foster the *Québécois* nation people and the First Nations, Inuit and Métis people, as well as her own natural children; it turns out she has a complex family to manage.

While we may be tempted to say more on behalf of the Native people—and certainly many areas of broken relationship between them and the French- and English-speaking members of the family have been documented—it is more appropriate that we listen to their own spokespersons and hear their own analysis of a pathway forward. The themes of lands and treaty rights, attempts to wipe out or assimilate their people and culture, separation of and from them by the settlers from the founding European peoples, various forms of abuse inflicted on them and governmental and other crimes, ineptitude and injustice in dealing with

Native people as groups, families and individuals all figure into a tragic story that only they have the right to tell to their victimizers and the world.

Given that the theme of this book is Reconciliation, however, it may be appropriate to note that the chosen means of dealing with the very specific government religious residential schools "chapter" in the First Nations relationship with other Canadian people is known as the *Truth and Reconciliation Commission*. As this book is being finalized early in 2008, the commission is getting underway as an attempt at justice and healing. From its name, one can infer that, as in Quebec's case, the story must first be truthfully exposed (this is in process, though some interference plays are still being run). Only after success in the truth phase might some processes leading to genuine reconciliation be initiated; hopefully these could open up into a transforming relational healing needed by the hurting blended family of Canada. Perhaps the big question is, "Will Canada be capable of walking the length of the truth and reconciliation trail in good faith?"

There are moves toward reconciliation with other First People worldwide. Both South Africa and Australia have made some progress.

Not all people interested in reconciliation in this context see it in the essentially Christian terms of *contrition* (repentance) and *forgiveness*. A more comprehensive approach might define it as taking mutually acceptable steps to move from antagonism to respect and trust. It is difficult to see how this can be done without acknowledging wrongdoing and then apologizing meaningfully enough so that it can be accepted and form a basis for a new relationship. To make it sufficiently transformative, a process of restorative justice may be needed, and some form of restitution may be part of that. At this point, if we want to go ahead with a genuine commitment to allow pertinent and lasting changes, it becomes evident that reconciliation can be costly to both victim and perpetrator as a comprehensive transforming transaction is negotiated and effected.

With this in mind, consider the following statement from Liz and Bert Genaille, First Nation people who offer their personal perspective on their historic, ongoing conflict with French and English Canadians. Bert speaks for them in the remaining words of this appendix:

242

BERT & LIZ GENAILLE,
DONALD AND LORRAINE'S GOOD FRIENDS AND COLLEAGUES

In the fall of 2001, I met Donald and Lorraine Gingras at Arlington Beach, Saskatchewan. Donald spoke about his personal journey and about Quebec. For the first time, I understood the background of French Canada and their desire to have a "distinct society." In my conversation with Donald, I told him I heard many stories about the French people talking about separating and other issues. I told him I used to say, "Why don't they cut off Quebec at the Ontario-Quebec border and push them into the ocean? They can have separation."

Looking from God's window, I found I was wrong in my attitudes towards Quebec. In Donald's testimony, he talked about reconciliation. He looked straight at me, a native, and said, "Bert, I am sorry for what we did to the Native people, invading and buying your land for trinkets." This was the first time I heard such a warm apology; I responded back to him, "I accept your apology. If it were possible, I would accept for all the Native people."

We have heard about Native people dealing with French and English Canadians to negotiate territorial rights and other painful issues from the past that are now exposed publicly. We have seen the government talking about buying peace through financial agreement or material compensation. And, as so many people observe, money alone cannot resolve the social and personal problems of my people. It is not more money, more power, and certainly it is not more isolation on our reserves that will resolve our issues. Donald's message of reconciliation reminds us that we are called for a greater purpose.

# BIBLICAL SCRIPTURES ON RECONCILIATION

⚜

Jesus, quoting from the Jewish prophet, Isaiah 61:1-2:

*The Spirit of the Sovereign LORD is on me, because the LORD has anointed me to preach good news to the poor. He has sent me to bind up the brokenhearted, to proclaim freedom for the captives and release from darkness for the prisoners, to proclaim the year of the LORD's favor and the day of vengeance of our God, to comfort all who mourn...*

Jesus, quoted in the Good News according to Matthew 5:23-24:

*Therefore, if you are offering your gift at the altar and there remember that your brother has something against you, leave your gift there in front of the altar. First go and be reconciled to your brother; then come and offer your gift.*

Paul, the Apostle of Jesus the Christ, in his letters to the Colossians 1:19-23:

*For God was pleased to have all his fullness dwell in him, and through him to reconcile to himself all things, whether things on earth or things in heaven, by making peace through his blood, shed on the cross. Once you were alienated from God and were enemies in your minds because of your evil behavior. But now he has reconciled you by Christ's physical body through death to present you holy in his sight, without blemish and free from accusation—if you continue in your faith, established and firm, not moved from the hope held out in the gospel. This is the gospel that you heard and that has been pro-claimed to every creature under heaven, and of which I, Paul, have become a servant.*

Ephesians 2:13-17:

*But now in Christ Jesus you who once were far away have been brought near through the blood of Christ. For he himself is our peace, who has made the two one and has destroyed the barrier, the dividing wall of hostility, by abolishing in his flesh the law with its commandments and regulations. His purpose was to create in him-self one new man out of the two, thus making peace, and in this one body to reconcile both of them to God through the cross, by which he put to death their hostility. He came and preached peace to you who were far away and peace to those who were near.*

2 Corinthians 5:17-20:

*Therefore, if anyone is in Christ, he is a new creation; the old has gone, the new has come! All this is from God, who reconciled us to himself through Christ and gave us the ministry of reconciliation: that God was reconciling the world to himself in Christ, not counting men's sins against them. And he has committed to us the message of reconciliation. We are therefore Christ's ambassadors, as though God were making his appeal through us. We implore you on Christ's behalf: Be reconciled to God.*

John, the Apostle of Jesus the Christ, in 1 John 4:7,11,16,18:

*Dear friends, let us love one another, for love comes from God. Everyone who loves has been born of God and knows God. Dear friends, since God so loved us, we also ought to love one another. God is love. Whoever lives in love lives in God, and God in him. There is no fear in love. But perfect love drives out fear....*

Jesus, quoted in the Good News according to John 6:37:

*All that the Father gives me will come to me, and whoever comes to me I will never drive away.*

What would stop you from wanting to be
reconciled with God?

The Lord is near to all who call him in truth.
He fulfills the desires of those who fear him.
He hears their cry and saves them.

God is waiting for you.

# BIBLIOGRAPHY

———————————— ⚜ ————————————

QUOTED BOOKS

Baird, Charles W. *History of the Huguenot Emigration to America*. Baltimore, Regional Publishing Company, 1966.

Bibby, Reginald W. *Restless Gods: The Renaissance of Religion in Canada*. Toronto: Stoddart Publishing, 2002.

Black, Conrad. *Maurice Duplessis*. Traduit de l'anglais par Jacques Vaillancourt. Montréal: Éditions de l'Homme, 1999.

Brunet, Michel. "The British Conquest: Canadian Social Scientists and the Fate of the *Canadiens,*" *Approaches to Canadian History*. Collection of texts prepared by Ramsay Cook, Craig Brown et Carl Berger. Toronto: University of Toronto Press, 1967. *Canadian Historical Readings*, no. 1: 84-98.

Canadian Automobile Association. *Heritage of Canada*. The Reader's Digest Association (Canada), 1978.

Choquette, Leslie. *Frenchman into Peasants: Modernity and Tradition in the People of French Canada*, Cambridge, Massachusetts; London, England, Harvard University Press, 1997, vii-397 p.

Cramp, J. M. *Les mémoires de Madame Feller*. Nouv. éd. St-Romuald: Éditions Beauport.

Duclos, Rieul P. *Histoire du protestantisme français au Canada et aux États-Unis*. 2 vol. Tome 1. Cap-de-la-Madeleine: Éditions Impact, 2003.

Duschesne, Pierre. *Jacques Parizeau: Le Croisé.* 2 vol. Tome I. Montréal: Éditions Québec Amérique Inc., 2001.

Fournier, Louis. *F.L.Q.: Histoire d'un mouvement clandestin.* Montréal: Éditions Québec/Amérique, 1982.

Frégault, Guy et Marcel Trudel. *Histoire du Canada par les textes (1534-1854).* 2 vol. Tome I. Éd. rev. et aug. Ottawa: Fides, 1963.

Garneau, François Xavier. *Histoire du Canada français.* Tome I. Genève: Éditions Famot, 1976.

Garneau, François Xavier. *Histoire du Canada depuis sa découverte,* Vol. 1. N. Aubin, Quebec, 1845-1846.

Gaudette, Michel. *Guerres de religion d'ici: catholicisme et protestantisme face à l'histoire.* Trois-Rivières: Éditions Souffle de Vent, 2001.

Groulx, Lionel. "Fleur de Lys." *Histoire du Canada français depuis la découverte: Le régime britannique au Canada,* 4e éd. Tome II. Montréal: Fides, 1960.

Lacoursière, Jacques. *Histoire populaire du Québec: Des origines à 1791.* 4 vol. Tome I. Québec: Éditions du Septentrion, 1995.

Lalonde, Jean-Louis. *Des loups dans la bergerie: Les protestants de langue française au Québec (1534-2000).* Montréal: Fides, 2002.

Larin, Robert. "Patrimoine." *Brève Histoire des protestants en Nouvelle-France et au Québec (XVIe-XIXe siècles).* No. 2. Saint-Alphonse-de-Granby: Éditions de la Paix, 1998.

Lemieux, Raymond et Jean-Paul Montminy. "Diagnostic." *Le catholicisme Québécois.* Québec: Éditions de l'IQRC, 2000.

Lougheed, Richard, Wesley Peach et Glenn Smith, dir. "Sentier." *Histoire du protestantisme au Québec depuis 1960: Une analyse anthropologique, culturelle et historique.* Québec: Éditions la Clairière, 1999.

Lougheed, Richard. *La Conversion Controversée de Charles Chiniquy: prêtre catholique devenu protestant.* Québec: Éditions la Clairière, 1999.

Lower, A.R.M. "Two Ways of Life: The Primary Antithesis of Canadian History." *Approaches to Canadian History.* Collection of texts prepared by Ramsay Cook, Craig Brown et Carl Berger. Toronto: University of Toronto

Press, 1967, "Canadian Historical Readings." No. 1: 15-28.

Murray, Iain H. *Revival and Revivalism: The Making and Marring of American Evangelicalism (1750-1858)*. Edinburgh: The Banner of Truth Trust, 1994.

Tessier, Yves. *Guide historique de Québec*, 3e éd. Québec: Société Historique de Québec, 1990.

Trudel, Marcel. *Initiation à la Nouvelle-France: histoire et institutions*. Montréal: Holt, Rinehart et Winston, 1968.

Trudel, Marcel. *Mémoires d'un autre siècle*. Montréal: Éditions du Boréal Express, 1987.

Vallières, Roger et Marc Beaudoin. "Pierre Dugua de Mons (1558-1628)." *Mouvement estrien pour le français*. http://www.mef.qc.ca/pierre-dugua- de-mons.htm. Consulté en ligne le 13-05-2004.

Vastel, Michel. *Trudeau le Québécois* Nouv. éd. Montréal: Éditions de l'Homme, 2000.

Vaugeois, Denis. *La fin des alliances franco-indiennes: Enquête sur un sauf-conduit de 1760 devenu un traité en 1990*. Montréal: Éditions du Boréal. Québec: Éditions du Septentrion, 1995.

Vinet, Lucien. *I Was a Priest*. Toronto: Canadian Protestant League, 1949.

Wade, Mason. *The French Canadians (1760-1945)*. Toronto: MacMillan Company of Canada, 1955.

## OTHER BOOKS

Bibby, Reginald W. *Fragmented Gods: The Poverty and Potential of Religion in Canada*. Toronto: Irwin Publishing, 1987.

Bibby, Reginald W. *Mosaic Madness: The Poverty and Potential of Life in Canada*. Toronto: Stoddart Publishing, 1990.

Fournier, Claude. *René Lévesque: Portrait d'un homme seul*. Montréal: Éditions de l'Homme, 1993.

Holmes, Arthur. *The Grieving Indian*. With the collaboration of George McPeek. Winnipeg: Indian Life Books, 1988.

Knowles, Paul, dir. *Sharing Your Christian Heritage*. Toronto: Mainroads Productions, 1982.

Langdon, Laurie. *Riding out the Storm in Quebec: A Biography of Les Barnhart.* (Bravant la tempête au Québec: Une biographie de Les Barnhart.) New Hamburg: L. G. Barnhart, 1997.

Lévesque, Raymond. *L'Amérique est un mensonge: Convictions, poèmes et chansons*. Recueil préparé par Sylvain Rivière. Québec: Éditions du *Québécois*, 2007.

Pohl, Rudy and Marny Pohl. *A Matter of the Heart: Healing Canada's Wounds*. Belleville: Essence Publishing, 1998.

Stibbe, Mark. *From Orphans to Heirs: Celebrating Our Spiritual Adoption*. Oxford: The Bible Reading Fellowship, 1999.

Twiss, Richard. *One Church, Many Tribes: Following Jesus the Way God Made You*. Ventura: Regal, 2000.

ARTICLES

Buzetti, Hélène. "Le projet de pays attendra encore au moins dix ans." *Le Devoir*. 23-24 juin 2007, p. A5.

De Gaulle, Charles. *Allocution prononcée au balcon de l'Hôtel de Ville de Montréal* (24-07-1967), Mouvement estrien pour le français. Accessed online, May 13, 2004, http://www.mef.qc.ca/charles_de_gaulle.htm.

De Grandpré, Hugo. "L'option souverainiste stagne ou régresse, selon 85 percent des Québécois." *Journal La Presse*. Montréal: 23 juin 2007, p. A2.

Gosselin, Gérard. "Le Québec, une société menacée dans ces fonde-ments: évolution de l'union libre, éclatement des ménages, avortement, dénatalité." Texte rédigé suite à une communication devant les membres et les invités du groupe Population et avenir, Paris le 28 avril 1999. Consulté en ligne le 28/02/2008. http://www.chastete-quebec.com/journal/08/assises.htm.

*Profil des familles et des ménages canadiens: la diversification se poursuit*. Statistique Canada. Série analytique du recensement de 2001. Accessed online, May 21, 2003. http://www12.statcan.ca/francais/census01/Products/Analytic/Index.cfm.

White, Patrick. "Quebec Separatist Dream Fades 25 years later." *Yahoo Canada News*. 15 Novembre 2001. Accessed online on November 19, 2001, http://ca.news.yahoo.com/011115/e2ap.html.

## WEB SITES

*Ministère des Relations avec les citoyens et de l'Immigration.* Gouvernement du Québec. Updated 2002, accessed May 13, 2004, http://www.drapeau.gouv.qc.ca.

*Site de la Nouvelle France,* http://www.sitenouvellefrance.com, Tel: 1-888-666-8027, e-mail: info@sitenouvellefrance.com

*Tadoussac: le poste de traite Chauvin.* http://www.tadoussac.com/FR/tourisme/musee.htm, Tel: 1-418-235-4657, e-mail: tadoussac@bellnet.ca

*"Donald has written an entertaining and yet scholarly book that has deepened my understanding, respect, and affection for the people and history of Quebec. But he has also pointed the way forward to a promising mountain-top future that can only be reached through hard work and honesty in the valley of reconciliation."*
**Dr. Rad Zdero, Ph.D, Biomedical researcher, conference speaker, author, Toronto.**

*"Sleeping Belle Province, how many more tears will have to run under the bridge of your sighs before the sweet kiss of reconciliation comes and gets you out of your sleep riddled with old dreams?"*
**Marie-Andrée Gagnon, Translator, editor, *Québécoise*.**

*"In a social context where diversity must include not only the celebration of our separate identity as a people group but also the ability to celebrate and show tolerance for others who differ from us, Donald, as a member of the French Canadian experience, shares with us the story of his own struggle to overcome the exclusion he felt so deeply and to create an honest reaching out to those other communities of exclusion with welcoming arms of embrace. His story opens a window of hope for us all, as we also seek to deal with this issue of diversity. I am grateful for how Donald's long twenty-year friendship has embraced me and enriched me as an Anglophone person and for his book that reflects him."*
**Dr. Bob Seale, Ph.D, theologian, professor, conference speaker, Caronport, Saskatchewan.**

## About the author

Donald Gingras has his first degree in Education and a MA in Family Counselling. He is married to Lorraine; they make their home in Montreal and have two children and six grandchildren. He has been a sports administrator and businessman, high school principal, conference speaker and missionary. He writes, "In this book you will learn what I experienced in Quebec as a French *Québécois* baby boomer. I have been an east Montreal altar boy, a teacher, a hockey coach...and a separatist! You will also read about a crossroad that transformed my life, through which I have been enabled to see and write this story from a wide-open window of hope."